Human Kind

True Stories to Restore Your Faith in Humanity

Shanaya Grant

Copyright © 2023 by Shanaya Grant

All rights reserved.

No portion of this book may be reproduced or used in any form without prior written permission from the author, except as permitted by U.S. copyright law.

ISBN 9798371479662

Although the author has made every effort to ensure that the information in this book was correct at press time, and while this publication is designed to provide accurate information in regard to the subject matter covered, the author assumes no responsibility for errors, inaccuracies, omissions, or any other inconsistencies herein, and hereby disclaims any liability to any party for any loss, damage, or disruption caused by errors or omissions, whether such errors or omissions result from negligence, accident, or any other cause.

Every ounce of optimism I have is from my brother and parents, so every word in this book is dedicated to them

Contents

Introduction 1
A New Kind of Fight 4
Seeing the Difference Volunteers Can Make 9
Made of Stone 13
An Entire Town Learns Sign Language 18
One Doctor 21
Homeless to Harvard 25
Twelve-Minute Drive 29
Hollywood Drop-Out 32
Pay-It-Forward Pizza 37
Can Fly, Even Without Arms 40
Braces, High School, and Breakthroughs 43
Kidneys for Home Runs 47
669 Children 51
Seven Summits, One Lung 57
Drone Deliveries 61
Patent the Sun 65
Man with the "Golden Arm" 68
The Friendship Bench... 71
Dr. Coffee 76
Strawberry Mansion 79
Happy Tails 85

Mama Rosie	88
You Gotta Have Heart	92
Veterans Who Surf	96
Fourteen Cows	99
Peter Pan's Everlasting Gift	103
Tangelo Park	106
Future Ties	110
Friends, Not Customers	113
Spider-Mable	118
Don't Judge a Book by Its Cover	122
Detroit Pioneer	125
Chocolate Bar	128
King Karma	132
Rolling Books	135
San Diego Highwayman	139
"James Bond of Philanthropy"	143
Music Mends Minds	147
Wales Fundraising	151
Human Race	154
The Street School	158
Adopt a Student	162
References	164

Introduction

Being human means many things, and one of the most beautiful is the ability to make choices. Every day, we have the choice to count our blessings. We have the choice to find ways to bring joy and happiness to others. We have the choice to manage our reactions. We have the choice to persevere. Although there are circumstances over which we have no control, the majority of our lives are the results of our actions and attitudes. We're all capable of helping someone, in some capacity, each and every day. We're all capable of making a positive impact on our surroundings.

It's easy to get wrapped up in the misfortunes that surround us through the media, but for every tragic news story, there are thousands of joyful ones. Yet, these heroic and inspirational stories often go unnoticed and without recognition. After all, a story about no wars breaking out or a global rise in literacy rates wouldn't make the evening news. It's crucial that for all the chaos and whirlwind of ominous reports being thrown at us, we don't construe a single selfish act to represent all of humanity.

We should strive to seek out the generosity, progress, and solutions that are constantly overtaking our world. This book is a collection of stories and research to prove beyond all doubt that people are inherently good and that none of us is too small or too busy to make a difference.

These true stories are of remarkable individuals exhibiting how extraordinary humankind is through their deeds and actions. The stories are theirs. I am merely the narrator, bringing their humanity to your attention.

"During my second month of nursing school, our professor gave us a pop quiz. I was a conscientious student and had breezed through the questions until I read the last one: What is the first name of the woman who cleans the school? Surely this was some kind of joke. I had seen the cleaning woman several times. She was tall, dark-haired, and in her fifties, but how would I know her name? I handed in my paper, leaving the last question blank. Before the class ended, one student asked if the last question would count toward our quiz grade. 'Absolutely,' said the professor. 'In your careers, you will meet many people. All are significant. They deserve your attention and care, even if all you do is smile and say hello.' I've never forgotten that lesson. I've also learned her name was Dorothy."

Chapter 1

A New Kind of Fight

Nine out of ten wins. An appearance on the television show *The Ultimate Fighter*. Justin Wren was dominating the mixed martial arts (MMA) fighting world. However, Justin's ongoing difficulties with depression and drug use quickly caught up to him, and he was kicked off one of the world's most recognized fight teams.

Justin had battled depression and bullying since he was a kid. The pills were a way for him to try to numb this pain, but it quickly spiraled out of control. In an attempt to get his life back on track, Justin started facing his addictions. He began volunteering at ministries and prisons to give back to others. It was here that he found a greater release from his pain than any pill or drink had ever supplied him. Helping others was starting to get Justin back to the person he knew he was.

Knowing there was more he could do before going back to professional fighting, Justin visited the Democratic Republic of the Congo (DRC) in Africa. The DRC has some of the richest resources, such as natural gas, but still struggles as one of the world's poorest countries.

The Pygmies are one of the inhabitants of the DRC who were neglected and malnourished. Justin soon learned that the Pygmies had been enslaved by neighboring tribes, forced to do grueling labor with only a few scraps of food in return. An average Pygmy was lucky to receive scrapings of goatskin hide to feed their entire family, and many of the children were stunted from malnutrition. It had even led to reports of cannibalism and massacres of these people by their neighboring slave masters. This group was labeled as "animals" or "the forest people" but often referred to themselves as "the forgotten people."

It was a blistering, humid day in the DRC when Justin was awakened by the sound of weeping tears. A mother was clenching her sick son, Andibo. Andibo was one of many Pygmies who had gotten ill from water-related parasites. The local doctors refused to treat him, stating that he was a "dirty Pygmy." Andibo's passing from an easily curable disease struck a chord with Justin. Someone had to help these people, so why couldn't he?

"I still love MMA, and my work with the Pygmies didn't change that, but it did change me. I'm not fighting for myself anymore. I'm fighting to bring attention and change to those who don't have a voice." – Justin Wren

Over the next four years, Justin continued to visit the DRC. One trip even lasted a full year where Justin slept in deep mud and prickly dirt. Justin came with monetary reinforcements and was able to buy over 2,000 acres of land for the Pygmies along with equipment to start drilling wells for water. The Pygmies were given programs to teach each other how to farm and survive on their own once again. For the first time in decades, these locals weren't forgotten. They felt like they belonged in a place that had made them feel worthless for so much of their history.

Justin Wren in Uganda with Batwa Pygmy children

"All of this was made possible because we really decided that we had to work through the locals. It was dependent on them [and] their investment into the project. So, we've hired on 18 locals...all we had to do was put the tools in their hands and the knowledge in their heads and send them out to be world changers because they're already hungry, eager, driven people who wanted to be the change in their very own country. They wanted to be the solution to their own problems." – Justin Wren

After a five-year hiatus, Justin returned to MMA fighting. He's stronger than he has ever been and has a new reason to compete. Justin continues to donate a portion of his earnings and all of his fighting bonuses to his foundation, which continues to help Pygmy tribes in the DRC, Uganda, and soon, other neighboring countries.

While some professional athletes' downtime is spent on trips to Malibu Beach or elite steakhouses, Justin continues to return to Africa and sleep in the depths of a damp forest. His family halfway across the world appreciates Justin's love to not only fight, but to also fight for others. If you ever find yourself lost, start by helping someone else find their way.

"You know what's cool about being blind?

There's no race.

I don't know people from beauty.

I know people from what comes out of their mouth, and what's in their heart.

That's how I know people.

It's very cool that way."

Chapter 2

Seeing the Difference Volunteers Can Make

Hans Jørgen Wiberg presented an idea in 2012 that would soon change the everyday lives of hundreds of thousands of blind people in over 150 countries around the world.

Hans is visually impaired and wanted a solution to help other people with vision problems. Hans recognized that sometimes the hardest thing about losing your vision is the everyday tasks that are taken for granted. That's how the idea of the Be My Eyes app was born. Be My Eyes is an app that allows volunteers to help the blind solve challenges. The app works by live-streaming a volunteer into the life of a blind person to help them see what they need to. Users tap a button on their phones when they encounter a challenge, which gives volunteers a notification that someone is requesting their help. The volunteer then has a live video connection with the user and can describe to them the information they can't see.

"We have decided that this needs to be a free service and we don't want to put ads all over the place, so we have found another way to make it into a sustainable business. We made Be My Eyes available for companies like Microsoft that want to help their blind customers.

Everybody wins only when nobody loses." - Hans Jørgen Wiberg

Think about your daily routine and how many activities require you to be able to read or see. Be My Eyes helps people read the expiration dates on their food, look up public transportation schedules, and shop for groceries. It makes everyday chores just a little bit easier.

"Now you can just be friends with your friends without having to ask them to do all kinds of favors for you." – Hans Jørgen Wiberg

The app also does more than just routine tasks. Users can have volunteers describe to them family photographs, what different colors are in their house, or the imagery and scenery of a destination. It's about more than just helping users get by; it's about enabling them to feel and understand the people and places around them.

One volunteer described her most rewarding Be My Eyes call, which she received from a woman getting ready for a date in Germany. The woman nervously described how she was going on a first date and didn't know what she would wear. The volunteer got to look through her closet and pick a beautiful dress for the occasion. The two ladies chatted afterward, and the volunteer was able to calm her nerves and give her the needed boost of confidence before the date.

"Sometimes I log off after eight to nine hours of work, and I feel like I've not really accomplished that much...but then I get these two to five minute phone calls from a Be My

Eyes user, and it's just great to be able to help. It's very rewarding, and all of a sudden, this frustrating day turns into a really great, rewarding, positive day." – Be My Eyes volunteer

With the help of millions of remarkable volunteers worldwide, Be My Eyes now offers assistance 24/7, and 90 percent of requests are linked with a volunteer in under 60 seconds. This is all possible thanks to the over six million volunteers who've downloaded the app.

If you are wondering where to start to make a difference and do some good with just the push of a button, look no further than Be My Eyes. Using this app can be done from the couch, so there are officially no excuses to not do something kind today.

"Bloodwork performed on soldiers showed that bodies are stressed by the perceived, not actual, difficulty of circumstances.

The brain does not want the body to expend its resources unless we have a reasonable chance of success. Our physical strength is not accessible to us if the brain does not believe in the outcome, because the worst possible thing for humans to do is to expend all of our resources and fail. If we do not believe we can make it, we will not get the resources we need to make it. The moment we believe, the gates are opened, and a flood of energy is unleashed.

Both hope and despair are self-fulfilling prophecies."

Chapter 3

Made of Stone

Every decision, thought, and moment was focused on soccer. Stone Kyambadde's whole childhood was spent training for and practicing the sport. Days began and ended with soccer. Stone sought out every opportunity he could find in Uganda to become better. As Stone became a teenager, he started getting attention across the country for his skills. He spent his whole life tirelessly pushing himself toward becoming a professional soccer player.

Stone started playing for regional teams until he was finally asked to play for the national Uganda team. He felt no one deserved it more. He had put every ounce of sweat, strength, and grit he had in him into getting here. To him, this was just the beginning. He dreamed of being asked to play all over Europe once the world saw what he could do on the field.

Early in his time with the national Uganda team, there was a close game that looked like Uganda was going to lose. Stone wasn't nervous. There was no one on the field who scared him. He was suddenly kicked the ball and saw an opening on the field. Stone had spent his whole life running through his training and knew there was no one who could beat him. While running the ball down the field, he suddenly felt a striking pain in the back of his knee. His body collapsed as he shrieked in agony. His leg felt like someone threw a brick at him. He lay on the field, struggling to remain conscious from the pain. As a stretcher took him off the field, he vaguely heard the referee call a red card on the opposing team. In that moment, Stone knew: the back of his knee had been kicked out. The injury had been done on purpose.

Stone worked to re-build his game, but his knee kept giving out. It was obvious that his soccer career had come to a rapid end and would never recover. His whole life and identity had been centered on the game. To have it taken away from him from an intentional injury was too much to bear.

This is where most people would have let bitterness overcome them. It would be easy to hate the game, the opponent who did this to you, and your unbearable luck. Yet, Stone took a different approach: he decided to stop thinking about the past and started thinking about what was next on his journey.

"I learnt that there is no future without forgiveness. Although I may not have fully understood it then, I know now that adversity can make you bitter or it can make you better.

I have learnt that when you choose to forgive, you open up many options for you to grow and change. I have learnt that disappointment can turn into a new appointment, if you are only open to it. If we choose not to forgive, we become victims and hold the future captive." – Stone Kyambadde

The one thing Stone had always known about himself hadn't changed: he loved the game. Using his passion, he started coaching children's soccer in Uganda. It started small, with a few kids from his neighborhood. Through word of mouth, his team quickly started to grow. The team was called the "Wolves."

Stone Kyambadde and the Wolves

The Wolves gained attention from all over Uganda, and not just from hosting some of the best players in the country, but from how Stone taught. Stone taught every player how to be a better man and give back to his community. With practices like a zero-tolerance policy on tardiness or fighting, Stone instilled discipline and kindness. Most Wolves players wouldn't become professional soccer players, but they would all become more responsible and capable citizens in Ugandan society.

"I have gone on to do greater things than would have ever been possible if I had just remained a player. I am more fulfilled in my life now because of all the work this new

direction has led me in. All the things in my life that have happened since are a product of me embracing a new life, a new world that was only opened to me after I was able to forgive, and move on." - Stone Kyambadde

"No one is useless in this world who lightens the burdens of another."

Chapter 4

An Entire Town Learns Sign Language

Being deaf and feeling like an outsider was a feeling that one resident of Bağcılar, Turkey knew all too well. Most people don't know sign language, so trying to communicate with others through hand gestures and pointing can be draining, frustrating, and make one feel like a constant annoyance.

A technology and advertising company came together to help deliver a gift to this resident: a day free from his everyday obstacles. The companies wondered if they could secretly teach sign language to the town of Bağcılar. When telling the town of their plan, the reaction was overwhelming. People of all ages took a pledge to take the time to commit to learning sign language, receiving nothing in return.

Residents gathered in crowds in the evenings and were taught by a teacher to communicate through hand gestures. Most of the locals had never even met the deaf resident, but that didn't stop them from wanting to help him. After hours of practice and studying, the town of Bağcılar started to grasp this new art of communicating.

On a sunny winter morning, the unknowing deaf resident got up and walked outside onto his sidewalk. He was immediately greeted by a passing local who signed "good morning." Continuing on to a local bagel shop, the cashier signed to him as he took his order and handled the payment. Starting to get confused, the resident continued onto the street to hail a cab. The cab driver pulled over to the side of the road and used sign language to say hello before taking him to the town center. The town, along with a camera crew, was excitedly waiting for the resident's arrival.

Taken aback, the resident got out of the cab. A member stepped forward and signed that the whole town had learned sign language just for him. The resident's eyes were overcome with a deep hue of red and tears started welling up. He broke into tears, in awe that a group of mostly strangers would take the energy, time, and commitment just to make his day easier. That was the first day when he no longer felt like an outsider in his own town.

"See if you can catch yourself complaining, in either speech or thought, about a situation you find yourself in, what other people do or say, your surroundings, your life situation, even the weather.

To complain is always nonacceptance of what is. It invariably carries an unconscious negative charge.

When you complain, you make yourself into a victim. When you speak out, you are in your power. So change the situation by taking action or by speaking out if necessary or possible; leave the situation or accept it.

All else is madness."

Chapter 5

One Doctor

Sudan's Nuba Mountains spread across 200 miles, are home to over one million people, and have only one major hospital and licensed doctor: Dr. Tom Catena. After decades of civil wars and bans on humanitarian aid to the region, Dr. Tom was an answer to thousands of residents' prayers.

Tom grew up in New York and attended Brown University, studying mechanical engineering. He was known around campus for more than just being on the football team; classmates recognized Tom for his distinctively warm and selfless nature. Tom went on to receive a medical degree from Duke University before becoming a flight surgeon in the United States Navy. It was here, working in the Navy, that Tom was sent to Kenya and fell in love with altruistic work.

In 2008, Tom packed up a few belongings, said goodbye to loved ones, and moved to the Nuba Mountains in southern Sudan. His first task was helping establish the Mother of Mercy Hospital, the only major hospital in the region. Since healthcare in the region was virtually nonexistent, Tom quickly filled the role of the only surgeon and skilled doctor for one million people.

A lack of medical professionals wasn't the only hurdle;

Human Kind | 22

the hospital often had to run without electricity, running water, or proper supplies. Tom figured out plans to help train others and use every ounce of medical knowledge he had learned to keep the 400-hospital-bed organization running at all times.

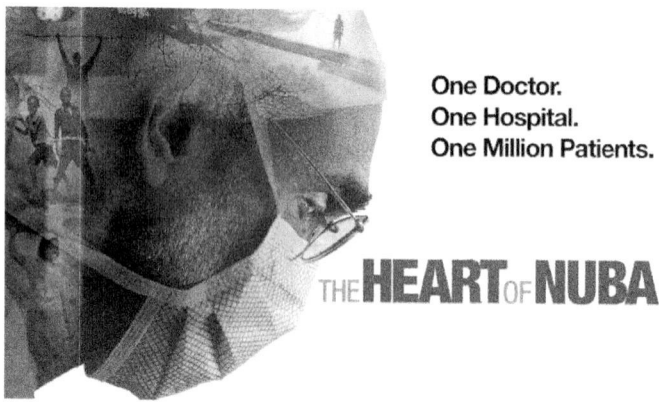

Image from the *Heart of Nuba* film released in 2016 about Dr. Tom Catena

Life in the Nuba Mountains was a sharp contrast with Tom's life in America. The continual fighting and bombings led to no place ever feeling too safe. The hospital is surrounded by foxholes, so when there are airplane bombings, patients and staff can flee to safety. Citizens have all come to dread the sound of propellers overhead, knowing explosions and terror are approaching. Tom also has to live without modern luxuries, any of his family, and only $350 a month. Despite these or any conditions, Tom remains resilient at the hospital he helped build.

"If I left, some people would die. So, I'm in it. I'm all in." – Dr. Tom Catena

In the over fifteen years Tom has spent in the Nuba Mountains, he has served as thousands of patients' gynecologist, surgeon, dermatologist, and everything in between. People from hundreds of miles know of Dr. Tom, and how much love and hope he has managed to instill. His 24/7 on-call medical expertise, warmth, and unwavering sense of humor continues to bring comfort to the thousands of people he now calls family.

"There was a reason I was born with so many positives, so many blessings. And I think it would be rather selfish to kind of take all that I was given from birth onwards and use that all for myself. There is some payback for me in this life. Not that I am suffering by any means now, but I think that giving something back is part of what we are expected to do...The lives of people here matter as much as everyone around the world. We can't lose sight of that, or else we lose our humanity." – Dr. Tom Catena

"A study [was conducted on] bankers right after the huge banking crisis hit. Most of them were incredibly stressed. But a few were happy and resilient. What did those guys have in common?

They didn't see problems as threats; they saw them as challenges to overcome...

We watched those groups of people over the next three to six weeks, and what we found was if we could move people to view stress as enhancing, a challenge instead of as a threat, we saw a 23% drop in their stress-related symptoms. It produced a significant increase not only in levels of happiness, but a dramatic improvement in their levels of engagement at work as well."

Chapter 6

Homeless to Harvard

No one had more of an excuse to complain than Khadijah Williams. From the age of six, Khadijah was homeless with her mother and sister in Los Angeles. Growing up, Khadijah was forced to move twelve times in twelve years due to unsafe conditions or their allowed time at a shelter expiring. Khadijah could have used this adversity to wallow in her misfortunes, but instead, she decided she had the power to make a change for herself.

In the third grade, Khadijah's scores on the state exam placed her in the 99th percentile. This meant only one percent of other students had scored higher than her. These results gave Khadijah confidence that she was gifted and capable, despite her living conditions. Education and learning were going to be her escape.

"People focus on the material things you don't have when you're homeless, but a lot of the challenge for homeless children is psychological. No matter how nice a shelter is, you never feel safe, and all you see around you are people who are down on their luck. It's not the kind of atmosphere that makes you think big. Books helped me escape all of that." – Khadijah Williams

In the following years, Khadijah's mother had to pull her out of school eight more times. Moving resulted in classes and even school years being missed. Khadijah took learning into her own hands. She read everything. From old cereal boxes, discarded magazines, to every book she could get her hands on. During one move, Khadijah had to wake up at 4 a.m. and take three buses in order to get to school. There was also extra work that needed to be done on her own to make up for all the courses she had to miss. If she was fortunate enough to sleep in a shelter and not on the streets, she would study in the hallway or bathroom after the lights went out. Books engulfed her attention in order to tune out the distractions from the hostile and intoxicated homeless folks surrounding her.

As a junior in high school, Khadijah had managed to not only be on pace with her fellow classmates, but she was also enrolled in advanced classes. With high school graduation approaching, Khadijah began applying to colleges. It was the moment she had been waiting and working so tirelessly for, as she knew education was her pathway out of poverty. She had gotten so used to hiding her grim upbringing that admitting she was homeless to college officials was a big deviation for her. Khadijah had never wanted her classmates to think she got special treatment or achieved an ounce of her success due to anything other than her hard work and intelligence. Now in college applications, she began to finally reveal to outsiders her living conditions and hurdles. These challenges were proof that she could continually achieve greatness, despite any barriers. Her unbelievable dedication allowed her to be accepted into 22 of the 26 top-tier universities she applied to, including Harvard.

Four years at Harvard was the longest that Khadijah had been in one place. She finally had her own bed, a consistent education, and a place to call home. These comforts only motivated her to work as vigorously as she had before. She could still be found most days and nights with her face wedged into a book.

Khadijah is now working in Washington, D.C., concentrating on enhancing public education. As difficult as reliving parts of her childhood is, she continues to share her story across the nation in case there's someone thinking they are too small or disadvantaged to achieve greatness.

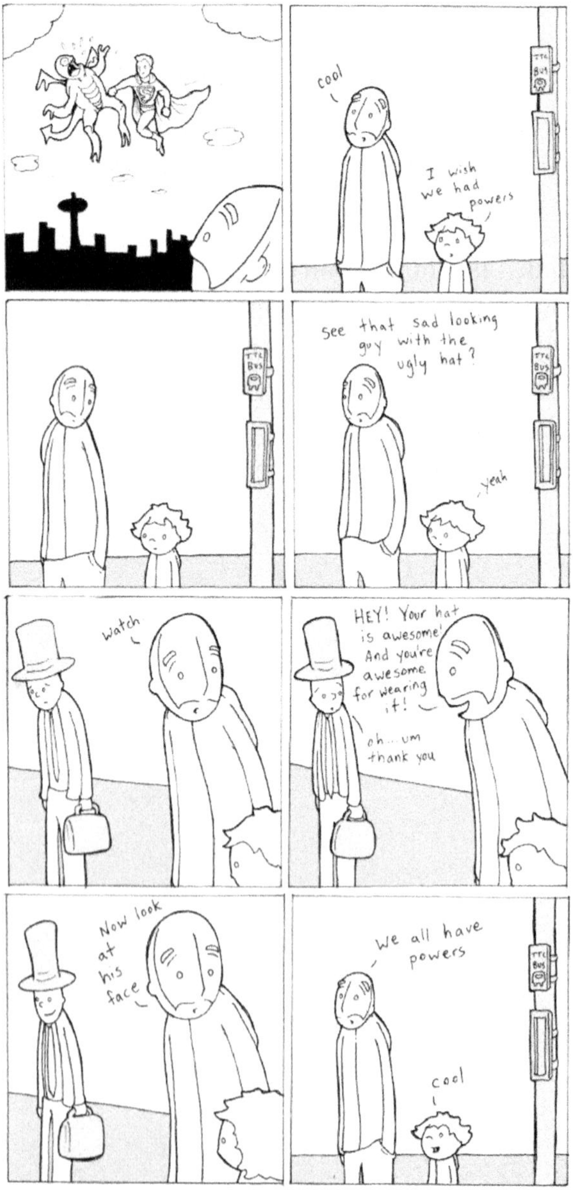

Human Kind | 28

Chapter 7

Twelve-Minute Drive

Between haircuts, waiters, and dentist visits, there are times when small talk is unavoidable. Most of the time, these encounters with strangers are fleeting and last just long enough to pass the time. A college student named Roland Gainer expected his upcoming Uber ride to be one of these brief encounters.

Roland was going to meet up with his friends when his cheery driver revealed he was driving in order to save money so his daughter wouldn't lose their house. His almost 70-year-old driver then announced he had been diagnosed with cancer and was expected to have between two and ten weeks to live. He was trying to quickly scrape up enough money so his daughter, a single mother, wouldn't lose the house they'd been living in.

That twelve-minute ride changed Roland's life. He knew he had a duty to help. Instead of letting his driver slip away, as happens with most strangers people come across, Roland made sure to get his name and number. Then, he began to get to work.

Roland started an online fundraising page to try raising the $90,000 that was required to keep the house. Within just one week, over 3,700 people and organizations had donated to raise over $100,000. The driver even insisted that since their goal was met, he would no longer accept another penny, as there are many others in the world who could use the help more now.

Who would have thought that one twelve-minute car ride to meet up with some college buddies would change so many lives? Thankfully, Roland took the time to live in the present and get to know someone.

"*Most of us spend too much time on what is*

urgent

and not enough time on what is

important."

Chapter 8

Hollywood Drop-Out

After 26 years in the film business, Scott Neeson found himself in need of a breather. Scott had been raised in a modest town in Elizabeth, Australia. After realizing school was not his forte, Scott dropped out of high school and started working a government-subsidized job at a drive-in movie theater. Here, Scott found he was drawn to the movie industry and began to work his way up the ranks. Years of devotion led Scott to Los Angeles, where he was later made President of 20th Century Fox International, one of the country's largest film studios. This job came with its perks, including a flashy mansion, invites to A-list parties, and a private yacht.

As envious as outsiders were of Scott's life, he found himself in need of a change of pace. When he accepted a new role with Sony Pictures Entertainment, he decided to take a five-week sabbatical before starting the position. He embarked on a trip to Southeast Asia and India. While in Cambodia, Scott wanted a cleanse from his Hollywood life, and made the unexpected request to see the worst poverty the country had to offer. He was led to a garbage dump in the city of Phnom Penh. It was the most toxic and unimaginable site Scott had ever seen.

The dump stretched across roughly 20 acres and was home to over 1,000 children who lived and worked upon it. Kids and families were rummaging through garbage under the 100-degree Fahrenheit sun merely to survive. Scott witnessed many kids who had been abandoned by their parents due to their not being able to afford them, or due to alcoholism or disease. It was a heart-wrenching catastrophe that Scott couldn't shake.

At the garbage dump, Scott met a young Cambodian girl covered in dirt, wearing scraps of clothing. Scott learned she didn't have any other clothes, and even if she did, she had nowhere to keep any belongings. It took Scott only 90 minutes to arrange plans to send her to a local school and find a place for her and her family to live. All Scott had to do was send her mother 35 dollars a month. With only 90 minutes and 35 dollars each month, Scott had forever changed a girl's life and broken her family's desolate cycle of poverty.

After five weeks, Scott returned home to his powerful job in Los Angeles. The impact a small amount of his time and money could make on the people in Cambodia was forever stuck in Scott's mind. He decided to return to Cambodia for a week each month.

Scott was living in two conflicting worlds. His life in Los Angeles was spent with a million-dollar salary, paparazzi, flashing lights, and awards shows. When he would return to Cambodia, he was overcome with sorrow and suffering.

On one of Scott's monthly trips to Cambodia, he received a phone call from a whining actor who had received the wrong amenities on his private jet. The actor pleaded that his life was too hard. Scott was standing with abandoned children fighting just to survive, and was suddenly overcome with clarity and certainty. After returning from that trip, he promptly quit his job and sold his house, boat, and most of his belongings, then moved to Phnom Penh.

"I thought there was something wrong with me. The more I got, the less happy I was." – Scott Neeson

The Cambodian Children's Fund was founded and became Scott's world. The not-for-profit helps children in Cambodia with a focus on education and healthcare. Scott started by supporting the children at the garbage dump. The fund's first concentration was the children's health, safety, and other immediate survival needs. As the Cambodian Children's Fund progressed, Scott focused on the whole system. He believed that opening free schools or healthcare wouldn't help the root of the problems, it would only mask it.

The schools require a high attendance rate and offer students courses that require critical thinking and leadership skills. Students are motivated to change their own community with programs to mentor each other, connect with the elderly, and feed other homeless children. The teachers at the Cambodian Children's Fund inspire these kids to be independent and bring change to their world. In return, these children and their families are provided with free schooling, transportation, and some housing and meals.

After five years, Scott and the Cambodian Children's

Fund's efforts resulted in the garbage dump finally being closed. After sixteen years, there are over 2,000 children enrolled in the free schools, 500 homes provided, and 30,000 people treated annually for free at the charity's local medical clinic.

The work and sacrifices Scott has endured have empowered thousands of children and created a ripple effect in the community. Scott has been able to see some of these children become lawyers and doctors, but more importantly, become more self-assured and empathetic individuals. Although Scott often misses the luxuries and comforts of his old Hollywood life, he claims that Phnom Penh is home, and these children are now his family and the deepest, rawest love he has ever felt.

Adam Rifkin's five-minute favor rule:

"You should be willing to do something that will take you five minutes or less for **anybody**."

Chapter 9

Pay-It-Forward Pizza

If you needed an excuse to go to a pizza shop guilt-free, Mason Wartman just gave you a great one. Mason was the owner of a restaurant in Philadelphia that sold one-dollar pizza slices.

Before opening his restaurant, Mason was working in the finance industry as an equity research associate on Wall Street. With the dream of always wanting to start his own business, he decided to bring New York-style pizza to his neighborhood in Philadelphia.

One particularly crowded evening, a customer asked if he could pay extra to cover the amount for a homeless person's pizza. Loving the idea, Mason quickly ran out of the store to buy a stack of sticky notes. He then stuck one of these lavender sheets by his cash register with a note saying that there had been one free slice purchased. Just like that, Rosa's Fresh Pizza's pay-it-forward restaurant began.

Customers soon flooded through the doors to buy an extra slice for someone in need. It was also a tradition for buyers to write motivational messages on these sticky notes.

Sticky notes left by customers at Rosa's Fresh Pizza

Thousands of free meals were distributed with an average of 80 people in need fed daily. Mason is proud to say many homeless individuals even bought free food for other homeless people. One customer, Eddie, used to be homeless and regularly came in to get free pizza. Eddie is now clean and has found a passion for working in insurance. Mason still keeps in touch with Eddie and so many others who have been able to turn their lives around and then come back to pay-it-forward to others in need. It became a rare place where people of all income levels and backgrounds felt welcome and happy to get to know one another.

"A little thing can change the world. Every great force in society was once discounted at its inception as too insignificant to make a difference." – Mason Wartman

"I think one of the most useless questions an adult can ask a child is...what do you want to be when you grow up?

As if growing up is finite. As if at some point you become something, and that's the end...

We don't know how time and circumstances will change what we want and even who we want to be, and locking our life GPS onto a single target can give us the right directions to the wrong destination."

Chapter 10

Can Fly, Even Without Arms

The thought of achieving multiple black belts in Taekwondo, becoming a pilot, and learning how to surf and rock climb might appear overly ambitious to a lot of people, but not to Jessica Cox. Jessica mastered all of this, and did so with no arms.

Jessica was born with no arms due to a rare birth condition. At age 14, she decided she didn't want to use prosthetic arms because she didn't want to hide who she was. All along, Jessica was faster and better at using her feet and other resources instead of prosthetic arms. Now determined, Jessica learned to drive a car, put in her contact lenses, and play the piano. There were no "ifs" for Jessica; determination and patience led her to always find a way.

With a childhood dream of learning how to fly a plane, Jessica set out on a quest to become a pilot. After years of training, Jessica received her pilot's license. She flew planes by using only her feet.

Becoming the first armless pilot wasn't enough for Jessica to stop pushing herself. She used this victory as momentum to further her Taekwondo skills, winning a state championship in a non-disabled competition. She won the fight with the help of her trainer and husband, whom Jessica met through Taekwondo.

Her extraordinary life started getting the attention of the media and other individuals with disabilities. Jessica realized the power she had to motivate others, and now gives motivational speeches in over twenty countries to encourage others to embrace their differences. Her speeches include her epiphany that her differences actually became her fiercest asset. Limitations are only the mental blocks you place on yourself.

"Handicaps are mindsets. Whatever it is that stands in the way of achieving something, that's when it's a handicap. I prefer to see them as obstacles or challenges. This is how I've been my whole life. I don't know any different. I just live my life through my feet." – Jessica Cox

"Intelligence seems like a strong contender as the key differentiating factor for the high-potential students. But it wasn't—at least not in the beginning. Why not?...

*The study was designed to find out what happened to students when **teachers believed** they had high potential. [The study] randomly selected 20 percent of the students in each classroom to be labeled as bloomers, and the other 80 percent were a control group. The bloomers weren't any smarter than their peers—the difference 'was in the mind of the teacher.'*

Yet, the bloomers became smarter than their peers... Some students who were randomly labeled as bloomers achieved more than 50 percent intelligence gains in a single year... The students labeled as bloomers continued to show gains after two years, even when they were being taught by entirely different teachers who didn't know which students had been labeled as bloomers. Why?

Teachers' beliefs created self-fulfilling prophecies. When teachers believed their students were bloomers, they set high expectations for their success. As a result, the teachers engaged in more supportive behaviors that boosted the students' confidence and enhanced their learning."

Chapter 11

Braces, High School, and Breakthroughs

Some teenagers' thoughts revolve around homework, friends, and what they're eating for dinner. Jack Andraka's thoughts revolved around inventing a novel cancer screening test. When Jack was 14 years old, a close family friend lost a battle to pancreatic cancer. The fact that there wasn't a reliable way to test early for pancreatic cancer frustrated Jack enough to want to do something about it.

Jack promptly consumed himself with researching and learning about pancreatic cancer biomarkers. Irritated teachers told Jack to stop and pay attention in class, and many of his peers thought it was a stretch that a 14-year-old could actually achieve this. Jack didn't listen.

For the next four months, Jack arranged test procedures for his theory. He detailed his procedure and timeline along with the needed budget and materials. He then proudly sent his well-thought-out theory to 200 cancer researchers. Jack quickly collected a lot of rejections, including some professors who mauled and tore apart Jack's work.

Weeks passed, and Jack had received 199 rejections. Jack didn't listen.

Ultimately, one professor at Johns Hopkins University

believed in Jack's theory and said yes. Jack's mom dropped him off at a lab after school and on weekends for seven months to test out his research.

"Youth aren't a problem, they're a solution... We're at an epitome of creativity and knowledge; we have these wild ideas, and we have enough knowledge to breathe life into them." – Jack Andraka

It was a sun-drenched spring morning in March when the streets suddenly filled with Jack's screeches of joy. His theories were passing all the preliminary tests and functioning without exception. Beaming with pride and pure bliss, he hurried out to his mom's car. Jack's test was able to identify abnormal levels of mesothelin, a protein formed in the early stages of pancreatic cancer. This would detect the illness while one was still in the initial and treatable stages of the cancer.

"You don't have to be a professor with multiple degrees to have your ideas valued. It's a neutral space, where what you look like, age or gender—it doesn't matter. It's just your ideas that count. For me, it's all about looking at the Internet in an entirely new way, to realize that there's so much more to it than just posting duck-face pictures of yourself online. You could be changing the world.

So, if a 15-year-old, who didn't know what a pancreas was, could find a new way to detect pancreatic cancer, just imagine what you can do." – Jack Andraka

Jack's work still has to go through years of extensive clinical trials before it can officially be approved and implemented. However, if all goes as planned, Jack estimates this test would be ten times more effective and roughly 26,000 times cheaper than the current pancreatic cancer test. Not a bad achievement for someone before they even have a driver's license.

"Consider this scenario.

You own shares in Company A. During the past year, you considered switching to stock in Company B, but decided against it. You now find that you would have been better off by $1,200 if you had switched to the stock of Company B. You also owned shares in Company C. During the past year you switched to stock in Company D. You now find out that you'd have been better off by $1,200 if you kept your stock in Company C. Which error causes you more regret?

Studies show that about nine out of ten people expect to feel more regret when they foolishly switch stocks than when they foolishly fail to switch stocks, because most people think they will regret foolish actions more than foolish inactions. But studies also show that nine out of ten people are wrong. Indeed, in the long run, people of every age and in every walk of life seem to **regret not having done things much more than they regret things they did***, which is why the most popular regrets include not going to college, not grasping profitable business opportunities, and not spending enough time with family and friends."*

Chapter 12

Kidneys for Home Runs

A good coach trains his players to play better. A great coach motivates his players. An extraordinary coach risks his life to help his players. Tom Walter was nothing short of an extraordinary coach.

Tom used to coach baseball at the University of New Orleans. When Hurricane Katrina hit in 2005, Tom took it upon himself to sacrifice his own needs and flooded house to first ensure his team was safe and relocated. When Tom transferred to Wake Forest University, his selfless nature was apparent to a new freshman baseball recruit who was making his decision on which college to attend.

While this new recruit was attending his last year of high school, he suddenly started to notice something wasn't feeling right. His energy levels had lowered, and he was losing weight every day. Doctors finally discovered that he had ANCA vasculitis, an autoimmune disease in which the body starts attacking its own healthy cells and tissue. The diagnosis came with a frightening result that his kidneys were quickly failing. The teenager's parents immediately got tested to see if they could donate a kidney, but they weren't a match. His brother was his last hope, but he sorrowfully learned his kidneys weren't a match either.

Without hesitation or having anyone ask, coach Tom Walter ran into the hospital to see if his kidneys were a match. On finding out he was eligible to donate to his player, he didn't look back.

"Preparing our players for life after baseball is the most important thing we do as coaches and educators.

Our goal is to help raise young men of kindness, empathy, and service. Our collective mission is to make an impact in the lives of those we touch. As the leader of our organization, it's my responsibility to set the ultimate example.

When I found out I was a match for Kevin, it was the easiest decision I have ever made." – Tom Walter

That Monday during practice, Tom told his team he was going to donate a kidney to help one of their teammates. This meant at least two months of recovery, and that's if everything went according to plan. The team went silent. Tom knew this operation could potentially jeopardize the team's success, and a sudden rush of panic came over him as he tried to anticipate their response. After a few moments of gripping stillness, the team broke out into celebration and a round of applause. Teammates were sprinting up the field to their coach to shake his hand and congratulate him. With that, Tom knew he had the seal of approval to donate his kidney.

The operation went smoothly. Both recovered fully and were able to play the sport they loved once again. The player receiving the kidney never could have expected this level of generosity and self-sacrifice from a baseball coach. Coach Tom Walter is the purest example of doing good without being asked for anything in return.

Rather than cursing the traffic delay,
hope that anyone in the accident is safe.

Chapter 13

669 Children

Sir Nicholas Winton isn't a household name, but there are not too many braver or more heroic role models. Nicholas was born in 1909 in London and worked at many banks before becoming a stockbroker at the London Stock Exchange.

At the age of 29, Nicholas had planned an elaborate ski trip to Switzerland when he abruptly altered his plans to visit Prague instead. A friend had urgently convinced him to come help assist in Jewish welfare work. It was the year before World War II broke out, and Czechoslovakia was in the midst of being occupied by Germany.

Upon his arrival, Nicholas discovered the vast number of Jewish families being displaced and sent to concentration camps. What struck Nicholas most were the children and their helpless fate when they were summoned to these Nazi camps. He took it upon himself to help as many endangered children as he could escape out of Czechoslovakia.

Nicholas set up a makeshift office at a corroded dining room table in his Prague hotel. The first step was figuring out where to take these children so they were safe and looked after. In order to bring the people to

Britain, they would have to go through the Netherlands. At the time, the Netherlands had border guards who would search trains for runaway Jewish travelers and return them to Germany. Nicholas managed to set up guarantees from Britain to cross through the Netherlands safely.

The next step was figuring out where to place these children in Britain. Nicholas worked tirelessly to find British families willing to put up money to welcome these kids into their homes. With the help of a few volunteers, including his mother, flyers were placed in newspapers, churches, and anywhere else around Britain that would allow them. Money started to come in, and Nicholas covered the remaining costs out of pocket.

Another hurdle Nicholas faced was proper documentation for these incoming children. There wasn't enough time to obtain all the proper documentation for everyone. Nicholas resorted to gaining access to forged documents and holding secret meetings to be able to collect enough paperwork to ensure everyone's safe arrival in Britain. There were many times when Nicholas had to resort to bribery and risky negotiations. The Nazis caught up to Nicholas and even started tailing him in Prague; this didn't slow down his efforts.

Parents were rushing into Nicholas's hotel room, begging him to take their children away to safety. They knew of their own cruel fates, but wanted their children to have a chance to survive this misery. Nicholas remembers the resilience it took as parents would smile and tell their kids they'd meet again soon, knowing the gloomy reality.

The first train of children departed from Prague safely. One of Nicholas's partners attested that Nazi and Czechoslovakian railway officials often had to be bribed, or they would seize all the children on board. Once the children reached Liverpool safely, Nicholas and his mother were there to greet them. A few of these children had family in the United Kingdom, but most went to live with strangers who were kind enough to open their doors.

With the first train a success, Nicholas and his partners organized as many trains as they could before Hitler invaded Poland and all borders controlled by Germany closed. Their efforts managed to allow eight trains to successfully carry these children to safety. Because of these eight trains, 669 children were saved.

One of the most heroic elements of Nicholas's story is what came after. Nicholas went on to lead a humble life, relying on his own hard work and not his past bravery to continue to better his career and the world around him. His story wasn't largely broadcast in the media until 50 years later when his wife found a dusty scrapbook in their attic. The scrapbook contained the names of the hundreds of children he rescued and the families that took them in. This book of "Winton's children" was then distributed, and many of the children whom he saved were located.

Pages from the scrapbook Nicholas created containing the children he helped save

In a BBC television special, Nicholas was invited to honor the work he'd done that had gone without major recognition for so much of his life. At the end of the program, the host asked anyone who owed their lives to Nicholas to stand. To Nicholas's surprise, dozens of people stood and started applauding loudly at the chance to thank the person who allowed them to be alive today. Children and grandchildren of the kids he helped save were invited to surprise him.

"If something isn't blatantly impossible, then there must be a way of doing it." - Nicholas Winton

Nicholas has since been honored by receiving a Knighthood from Queen Elizabeth II, receiving the Order of the White Lion from the Czech Republic, having multiple documentaries made of his efforts, and having statues and trains devoted to him. However, Nicholas isn't remembered by any award; he's remembered for recognizing when others needed help and knowing the power of being a shining light even in the darkest of times.

"The optimist believes that bad events have specific causes, while good events will enhance everything he does; the pessimist believes that bad events have universal causes and that good events are caused by specific factors."

Chapter 14

Seven Summits, One Lung

Defying odds is what Sean Swarner is best known for and is what led him to climb 29,000 feet up Mount Everest. Defying odds is how he did this while being a two-time cancer survivor.

Sean was playing a game of pick-up basketball at age 13 when he tripped and fell to the pavement. Expecting a bruised knee, Sean was shocked when his whole body started to swell up. Doctors determined this wasn't a natural reaction to a casual fall and started doing tests, only to find that Sean had cancer. It was stage four Hodgkin's lymphoma, and was so aggressive that Sean was given three months to live. Sean credits his naiveté for the strength and optimism to prove his doctors wrong. After one year of grueling chemotherapy, doctors declared Sean cancer-free.

A few years later, during a routine check-up, Sean was told the cancer had resurfaced. The cancers were completely unrelated, and this cancer, Askin's sarcoma, was even more fatal. Doctors now gave the 16-year-old a six percent chance of survival with two weeks to live. Sean noted that it was more likely someone would win the lottery four times in a row with the same numbers than to have survived both cancers. But survive, he did.

After Sean beat these incredible odds, he felt compelled to live his life to the fullest and inspire others diagnosed with cancer. Sean started his own non-profit, the CancerClimber Association, which funds cancer research and awards adventure grants to other cancer patients looking for hope. He then made up his mind that he wanted to be the first cancer survivor to climb Mount Everest, the planet's highest mountain. There was one catch: Sean only had one working lung. During his second bout of cancer, his right lung suffered irreparable damage from the radiation treatment. This made Mount Everest guide companies reluctant to accept Sean as a client. To make matters more difficult, Sean didn't have enough climbing experience. He had trained with his brother on Mount Elbert in Colorado, but this was about twice as low as Mount Everest. Yet, Sean had managed to raise enough money for the climb, and now he was determined to find a way to make it up there. Eventually, National Geographic agreed that Sean, one cook, and two Sherpa could do the climb on their permit.

The battle to climb Mount Everest was grueling, demanding all of Sean's positive mental power and determination to succeed. If there was even one second where he had stopped believing he could achieve the climb, he wouldn't have made it.

As soon as Sean made it back down the peak, he began working on his next endeavor. His next mission was to climb the rest of the Seven Summits. The Seven Summits are the highest mountain peaks in Africa, Asia, Australia, Europe, South America, Antarctica, and North America.

Sean managed to climb all of these, becoming the first cancer survivor to achieve this feat as well. Not done with what he could do with one working lung and two near-death cancer afflictions, Sean also completed the Hawaii Ironman. The Hawaii Ironman includes a 2.4-mile swim, a 112-mile bike ride, and a 26.2-mile run.

Sean spends his energy now focusing on his non-profit and inspiring others battling cancer and other illnesses. He is an international keynote speaker and creator of the Summit Challenge. Sean encourages others to recognize the power their mind plays in determining their future.

"So many people are fixated on what's comfortable. Life begins outside your comfort zone, but fear holds them back." – Sean Swarner

"On average, the number of people living in extreme poverty declined by 47 million every year since 1990."

On any average day, the number of people in extreme poverty declined by 100,000+ people.

Chapter 15

Drone Deliveries

Rwanda faces a constant struggle to provide their millions of residents with access to timely medical supplies. Hospitals can't afford or lack the infrastructure to maintain their own refrigerated supplies, so rely on those materials to be transported to them.

Former college roommates, Keller Rinaudo and Will Hetzler, learned of a Rwandan database of emergency medical supply requests by doctors that had gone unfulfilled or were too late in arriving. The duo noticed an opportunity to halt the mass amounts of curable disease deaths taking place.

Keller and Will were aviation and robotics experts who launched the concept of delivering these supplies to hospitals via drones. Their vision was to house a distribution center with medical supplies in a central location in Rwanda. Drones would fly from this center to the hospitals and make the deliveries.

In 2016, a mother held her sobbing two-year-old, Ghislane. Ghislane had malaria and the doctors' last resort was to give her a blood transfusion. However, the central blood bank would take hours to reach, and Ghislane didn't have that long. Instead, a doctor sent a text message detailing the red blood cells that were needed. In less than 10 minutes, a drone flew in and dropped off the request. Ghislane's life was saved, and she became the first person to receive these medical supplies through drone delivery.

"I used to see the drones fly and think they must be mad, until the same drone saved my life." - Alice Mutimutuje, mother in Rwanda

The company, called Zipline, is revolutionizing healthcare in rural areas. The drones fly every day, in all weather conditions. It now takes just minutes for an order to be delivered at hospitals and is ordered with a tap of a button through their app. Zipline reaches over 25 million people in Rwanda and Ghana and flies more than 40,000 kilometers, the total circumference of the Earth, every week.

The success of Zipline has led to another distribution center being opened in Rwanda and four centers opening in Ghana. Each of these centers can make 500 deliveries every day. Children near the centers come to cheer on the drones as they launch into the sky, racing to save lives.

Zipline is not only saving lives by providing blood and other routinely needed products, but by allowing access to rarely used medical supplies. Items like frozen plasma and platelets require unique freezers and aren't stored by rural hospitals. Now, millions of patients who require special products can receive these items in just minutes at their local hospital.

Keller and Will continue to expand their reach with their

ultimate goal of providing every person in the world with timely access to medical products.

"5.8 million kids die every year due to lack of access to basic medical products. When we heard that, especially in a world with as much wealth as we have, it seemed completely insane to us that no one had applied technology to solve this problem once and for all. We don't think the exciting potential for that technology is delivering burritos or pizza. We think the exciting potential for that technology is providing universal access to healthcare to every human on the planet." – Keller Rinaudo

"Most important of all, we should be teaching our children humility and curiosity.

Being humble, here, means being aware of how difficult your instincts can make it to get the facts right. It means being realistic about the extent of your knowledge. It means being happy to say, 'I don't know.' It also means, when you do have an opinion, being prepared to change it when you discover new facts.

It is quite relaxing being humble, because it means you can stop feeling pressured to have a view about everything, and stop feeling you must be ready to defend your views all the time."

Chapter 16

Patent the Sun

In the mid-19th century, polio was a dreaded disease that kept people around the world up at night with fear of contracting it. There were deadly outbreaks of polio cases that swiftly affected thousands of people, particularly impacting children. No cure or prevention was known for this disease, and the death toll seemed to be escalating daily. Jonas Salk took it upon himself to end this global epidemic.

Jonas got into medical school in the 1930s and was the first in his family to go to college. He then focused his energy on researching viruses. He developed a vaccine that he believed could stop the polio virus. Eager to start distributing his vaccine, he immediately started the trial phase. Jonas was so confident in his work that he even had himself injected during clinical trials. After extensive testing from millions of willing participants, Jonas's vaccine proved effective in creating antibodies.

A natural next step after creating a cure for a cruel disease might be to patent your invention in order to reap the financial rewards. However, Jonas had a different approach. As soon as his vaccine was approved, he firmly stated he didn't want to even consider a patent. Jonas believed his discovery belonged to the people, not himself. The monetary value of this medical breakthrough could have been worth billions of dollars, but Jonas intended to keep costs low and was more focused on distributing his vaccine than being rewarded from it.

Jonas went on to create his own foundation, Salk Institute for Biological Studies, and continued to research viruses. He is globally recognized as the man who helped curb the spread of polio while ensuring his vaccine was vastly distributed, forgoing the opportunity for his own wealth. When asked in an interview who owned the patent for the vaccine, Jonas replied:

"Well, the people, I would say. There is no patent. Could you patent the sun?" – Jonas Salk

"Our first waking thought of the day is 'I didn't get enough sleep.' The next one is 'I don't have enough time.' Whether true or not, that thought of not enough occurs to us automatically before we even think to question or examine it...

We're not thin enough, we're not smart enough, we're not pretty enough or fit enough or educated or successful enough, or rich enough-ever. Before we even sit up in bed, before our feet touch the floor, we're already inadequate, already behind, already losing, already lacking something. And by the time we go to bed at night, our minds race with a litany of what we didn't get, or didn't get done, that day... What begins as a simple expression of the hurried life, or even the challenged life, grows into the great justification for an unfulfilled life...

We have the choice in any setting to step back and let go of the mind-set of scarcity. Once we let go of scarcity, we discover the surprising truth of sufficiency. By sufficiency, I don't mean a quantity of anything...It is an experience, a context we generate, a declaration, a knowing that there is enough, and that we are enough...

It is a consciousness, an attention, an intentional choosing of the way we think about our circumstances."

Chapter 17

Man with the "Golden Arm"

James Harrison's somber life in Australia quickly took a turn when he was rushed into the emergency room at age 14 and had to have one of his lungs removed. The operation forced James to receive almost two gallons of donated blood in order to survive. At a young age, James realized the only way he survived was through the generosity of others' blood donations. He decided he had to give back, too.

Donating blood seemed like an obvious way for James to help others, so once he turned 18, he started to give back. Doctors were quickly startled by an exceptional facet in the blood he was donating, a facet that could save lives. James's blood seemed to have a rare antibody named Rh (D) immune globulin. This antibody has the ability to fight an illness called Rhesus disease. Rhesus disease affects pregnant women and is where an unborn baby's blood cells are attacked by their mother's blood. The blood James was donating was able to stop this disease and ensure a healthy baby was delivered.

The medical community speculates that James has this antibody due to his blood transfusion at age 14, but no one knows for sure. All they know is that James had the ability to save lives, and that's exactly what he did.

"Fifteen minutes of your time could be a lifetime for somebody else." – James Harrison

James donated blood for over 60 years, until the age of 81. His plasma donations went from every eight weeks to six weeks, then to four weeks, then to three weeks, and finally, to every two weeks. To date, James has donated more than 1,100 times. According to the Australian Red Cross, James's donations have saved the lives of over two million babies. Quite a difference made by one individual.

Although not everyone might have this extraordinary "golden arm," many still have the ability to donate blood. The American Red Cross estimates 38 percent of people in the United States are eligible to donate blood; however, less than 10 percent of these eligible people actually do so each year.

"The life you save could be your own." – James Harrison

"The University of Warwick and the University of Manchester...compared large data sets where 1000s of people had reported on their well-being. They then looked at how well-being changed due to therapy compared to getting sudden increases in income, such as through lottery wins or pay rises...

They then showed that the increase in well-being from an £800 course of therapy was so large that it would take a pay rise of over £25,000 to achieve an equivalent increase in well-being.

The research therefore demonstrates that psychological therapy could be 32 times more cost effective at making you happy than simply obtaining more money."

Chapter 18

The Friendship Bench

One in a million. That's about the ratio of how many trained psychiatrists there are for the population in Zimbabwe. One of these handful of psychiatrists is Dr. Dixon Chibanda, who saw a daunting problem with the country's lack of mental health assistance. There was also the added stigma of getting treated for mental illnesses in Zimbabwe. In 2006, Dixon decided to start by using community grandmothers, known locally as Ambuya Utano, to help be the therapists the country desperately needed.

Dixon started training these local grandmothers in evidence-based talk therapy and behavioral activation. Why grandmothers? After extensive research of different demographics, Dixon felt they were best suited as they lived and worked in the same society, so they understood the community more than outsiders. They are also highly respected, the traditional holders of wisdom, and the most trusted to be able to uphold confidentiality.

There were park benches set up around the city in Harare, Zimbabwe. These places became safe spaces for people suffering from mental health illnesses to come and speak with a trained grandma in the community.

A Friendship Bench session in Harare, Zimbabwe

Grandmothers are taught to listen, show empathy, and allow people to speak their truth. Individuals meet with the grandmas every week on the bench for six weeks. Sessions include listening to people's stories and struggles, problem identification and exploration, and goal-setting. Grandmothers check in frequently with members and make home visits as needed. After individual sessions, members are invited to join Circle Kubatana Tose (CKT) sessions. Circle Kubatana Tose stands for *holding hands together* and are group therapy sessions for the neighborhood. CKT gatherings allow people to openly discuss their journeys, and they are taught to crochet items from recycled plastic so they can generate an income and discover purpose and belonging. Confidentiality is stressed, and members stand quietly while others are sharing. These sessions not only continue to provide group therapy, but also help break down the mental health stigma in the community.

News of the friendship benches spread quickly throughout Harare, and the idea has been implemented in cities all over Zimbabwe. The concept soon took root in other African countries and North America. The model has also expanded its focus, now opening at universities and focusing on loneliness as well as mental health.

"My big dream is to see the Friendship Bench thrive in every country. I'd like to see that everyone everywhere has someone to talk to... Another...important thing is that it's not just a place for treatment. We prefer to look at it as a place that helps to create space for healing, because that's what most people need. A space to address loneliness. Even in the developed world, loneliness has become an epidemic.

Not everyone who comes to the bench meets the diagnostic criteria of depression, they are simply lonely. Humans all over the world yearn for acceptance and human contact and that is provided on the bench, no matter where they are." - Dixon Chibanda

People seemed skeptical of Dixon's idea until the research started shedding light on how impactful these benches could be.

A clinical trial was conducted on almost 600 randomized patients in Zimbabwe. Half the patients received treatment from the grandmothers through the friendship bench. The other half received standard treatment from mental health professionals. After six months, results found that patients who were sent to the friendship bench had fewer mental illness symptoms than when they received treatment from standard mental health specialists. Experts have argued over why these benches have such a strong positive impact, but all can agree that these grandmothers are revolutionizing mental health in Zimbabwe.

Traveling and exploration keeps us healthy.

Research shows that travel provides the same physical and cognitive benefits as reading newspapers, crossword puzzles, or museum visits.

Traveling also leads to increased mood and outlook (86%), lower stress levels (78%), and improved physical well-being (77%).

Chapter 19

Dr. Coffee

The 2010 earthquake that hit Haiti has been long forgotten by many, but not by Megan Coffee. Megan received her medical degree from Harvard and doctorate from Oxford University before working a prestigious research position. Megan dropped her enviable job and former life when she heard about the damage caused by the earthquake in Haiti. Millions of people had been affected and weren't getting proper healthcare treatment. There wasn't enough money, resources, or doctors to help combat infectious diseases, such as tuberculosis and HIV.

Megan flew down to Port-au-Prince, Haiti, and started attending to the suffering Haitians. As soon as Megan stepped off the plane, she immediately recognized there was a substantial amount of medical support needed. This spurred Megan to establish her own tuberculosis clinic, which began with one Haitian nurse in a tent.

Weeks passed, and volunteering nurses and doctors from around the world started heading home, but not Megan. There were still thousands of people without the money or resources for treatment, so Megan expanded her clinic.

She would even spend her own money and fundraise to

scrape up food and supplies for those she treated. Soon, this hospital would treat over 4,500 people.

A twelve-hour day, seven days a week schedule became the norm for Megan. She spent four strenuous years living and caring for as many of the locals as she could. Megan didn't do this for any reward; in fact, she didn't even get paid. She gave up her well-off research position in the United States in order to work a grueling job for zero pay. Megan was provided housing and relied on donations for meals.

Megan's goal is to put herself out of work by stopping these infectious diseases. She has selflessly donated her life to improving others' lives, and continues to split her time between Haiti and other places in need of infectious disease care and interventions. Dr. Megan Coffee remains a hero for not only the vast impact she's had, but for healing and saving lives for pennies in return.

"10% of life is made up of what happens to you. 90% of life is decided by how you react...

We cannot stop the car from breaking down. The plane will be late arriving, which throws our whole schedule off. A driver may cut us off in traffic. We have no control over this 10%. The other 90% is different. You determine the other 90%. How?

By your reaction."

Chapter 20

Strawberry Mansion

Heavy metal chains were wrapped around the front entrance. Once inside, dusty hallways with dim lighting led you to the classrooms. Classrooms were filled with broken furniture, outdated textbooks, and stacks and stacks of old papers. Back offices were piled with thousands of unused materials and resources. This was not a school.

As Linda Cliatt-Wayman looked around Strawberry Mansion High School, she noticed the classrooms were nearly empty. Lockers were unfilled and left open. Teachers, out of fear for their own safety, taught with little to no expectations. Fights broke out regularly in every corner of the building. This was not a school.

It was Linda's first day as principal, and she was the fourth new principal in four years. She sat down with the teachers, who listed all their complaints. Only 68% of the students regularly came to school. 100% of students came from poverty. Parent participation was at 1%. 39% of students had special needs. 6% of students were proficient in algebra and 10% were proficient in literature. The statistics on why they were bound to continue failing went on and on. Finally, when the teachers were done venting about the problem students and their doomed cycle, Linda steadily responded with,

"So what? Now what? What are *we* going to do about it?"

Linda was no stranger to low-income education. Growing up, she had attended an impoverished high school not far from Strawberry Mansion in Philadelphia. Luckily, Linda had a strong mother, who challenged and pushed her through school. Fueled by the injustices she saw growing up, Linda went on to teach special education for 20 years and held previous principal and superintendent roles before coming to Strawberry Mansion. Linda was used to the struggles of poor schools, but this was a new challenge. Strawberry Mansion had even been registered on the top list of "persistently dangerous" schools in America for five consecutive years. The place Linda saw on her first day was not a true school where children were learning and flourishing. But Strawberry Mansion only fueled her motivation.

It started with small fixes. The gloomy lighting was replaced with bright lights over hallways and classrooms. All locker codes were hand reset so students could have a safe place for their belongings. Every inch of wall space in the building was filled with art, color, and uplifting notes. Classrooms were cleaned of outdated materials, broken furniture, and garbage. The heavy metal chains were removed from the front entrance.

Linda and her team worked tirelessly to clean and fix up the school. Once the school looked worthy, it was time to make it feel worthy. The school's budget was rebuilt from scratch to allocate more money toward additional support staff and teachers. The school day's schedule was revised to include honors courses, remediation, counseling, and extracurricular activities, all during school hours. A discipline program was implemented for all students in an effort to promote positive behavior. Results from these changes came steadily, and eventually resulted in Strawberry Mansion being removed from the list of "persistently dangerous" schools.

Despite all the progress in lowering crime and increasing attendance, Linda knew her team's job was just getting started. In order to have a long-lasting impact on these students and the students to come, they needed to have role models, support, and a desire to learn. No excuses on why this couldn't be achieved were tolerated. An emphasis was placed on teachers; not what was being taught, but how it was being taught. There was a push toward small group instruction so students of different capabilities could get their distinctive requirements met in the classroom. The teachers also had the ability to get to know the students on a deeper and more personal level. This element was vital due to the students' lack of parental involvement and encouragement. After just one year of the small group instruction, there was a 171% growth in algebra scores and a 107% growth in literature scores.

While all the progress was being made, Linda made it her personal mission to get to know the students. Her school days were not spent in her principal's office; rather, Linda would walk the halls and get to know each of the faces she passed. She would belt out "happy birthday" on students' birthdays. Every afternoon was spent in the cafeteria, where she would talk to the students. She would hear stories of incarceration, growing up with no parents, gangs, and hunger. Stories that many students had never had the nerve to tell, or someone willing to listen. This mattered; they needed to feel heard, understood, and important in order to understand their potential and how education could help. There were monthly town halls, where students could also tell their stories or talk about the changes they'd like to see in the school. It was Linda's job to listen. It was Linda's job to care.

"When I look at them, I can only see what they can become and that is because I am one of them. I grew up poor in North Philadelphia, too. I know what it feels like to go to a school that is not a school. I know what it feels like to wonder if there is ever going to be any way out of poverty. But because of my amazing mother, I got the ability to dream, despite the poverty that's around me. So, if I'm going to push my students toward their dream and their purpose in life, I got to get to know who they are. So, I have to spend time with them...every moment is a teachable moment." – Linda Cliatt-Wayman

Through all the stories and singing, Linda was strict. Rules were non-negotiable, and there were stringent consequences for every skipped class, brawl, or missed assignment. Every day on the morning announcements, Linda would preach the rules and core values of Strawberry Mansion. Students were reminded of how education is how they could change their lives. Every announcement ended with one of Linda's favorite and most renowned lines: "If nobody told you they loved you today, remember I do, and I always will."

"If we are truly going to address and make real progress in addressing poverty, then we have to make sure that every school that serves children in poverty is a real school. A school that provides them with knowledge and mental training to navigate the world around them." – Linda Cliatt-Wayman

This was now a school.

"The problem is that **'by now'** is a phrase we say to ourselves when we're trying to believe the lie that it's too late to start pursuing our dream."

Chapter 21

Happy Tails

Fulfilling the dream of millions of software engineers, Rakesh Shukla was able to start and run his own software company in Bangalore, India. His company boomed, giving Rakesh and his wife the opportunity to live a luxurious life filled with lavish cars and traveling to each end of the earth as many times as they wished. Although there was wealth and fame, something was missing in Rakesh's life that he only discovered one morning when Kavya came pouncing into his life.

Kavya was a two-month-old Golden Retriever that captured Rakesh's heart and provided the answer to his lifelong question of his purpose in life. Just a few months later, Rakesh brought home Lucky, a rescue dog he found damp and shivering in a ditch on the streets. Soon, one rescue dog turned into two, which turned into twenty. Knowing Rakesh didn't have the space or resources at his home to care for so many dogs, he bought land and opened a farm for the animals to happily reside.

The farm became Rakesh's second self-started company, called the Voice of Stray Dogs. Rakesh acknowledged how many of these strays and rescues needed medical treatment, so he hired veterinary assistants, chefs, and caregivers. The farm has rescued over 8,000 abandoned dogs and is one of the largest rescue facilities in the world. Any dog, no matter the age or sickness, is accepted.

The Voice of Stray Dogs has done so much to help stray dogs, and now extends to ex-military dogs. When Rakesh learned that many retired army dogs were being sent to live the remainder of their lives in crowded kennels, he decided he had the power and purpose to change this. These dogs had been trained since the age of two months to perform search and rescues, uncover explosives, and protect bases. That sort of dedication and heroism deserved a happier ending. Rakesh started rescuing and transitioning these military dogs from a life of work to a domestic retired life they'd earned. Wags all around.

"About success, I know now it is not the multiple houses and cars and watches and visas I thought it did. It is having the means and the opportunity to spend each day doing what you love." – Rakesh Shukla

Harvard conducted one of the world's longest adult studies to see what brings people happiness. In the 1930s, 724 teenagers were selected to collect data from year over year for 80+ years. Later, thousands of their children were also introduced to the study as well. The universal findings?

"Good relationships keep us happier and healthier. Period...

Social connections are really good for us... It turns out that people who are more socially connected to family, to friends, to community, are happier, they're physically healthier, and they live longer than people who are less well connected...

When we gathered together everything we knew about them at age 50, it wasn't their middle-age cholesterol levels that predicted how they were going to grow old. It was how satisfied they were in their relationships. The people who were the most satisfied in their relationships at age 50 were the healthiest at age 80.

It's not just the number of friends you have, and it's not whether or not you're in a committed relationship, it's the quality of your close relationships that matters."

Chapter 22

Mama Rosie

Rosie Mashale didn't expect much to change except her address when she and her husband moved to Khayelitsha in South Africa. Every morning, Rosie would hear the playful screams and chatter from a group of kids playing at a local plot of land near their new home. Confused, Rosie finally decided to step outside and ask one of the children what they were doing there.

Learning that these children had been left by their mothers during the day, Rosie took them to her house. These children's parents were mostly single mothers who spent the day working or looking for work, and didn't have a place to leave their children during the day. Rosie gave them food to eat and sang rhymes with them all day. When their parents learned of Rosie's kindness, they pleaded with her to keep their children every day. Rosie promptly gathered other stay-at-home neighbors to help, and they were quickly responsible for the care of 36 local children. Thus became the start of Rosie's Baphumelele Educare Centre (baphumelele translates to *we have progressed*).

After a year, Rosie was in need of a mindful break and decided to take a yearlong sabbatical. Shortly into this break, Rosie came home one day to find a screaming child on her doorstep. He was covered in dirt and bruises, and couldn't even remember his own name. Rosie quickly took him into her home and bathed and fed him before taking him to the police station. Instead of taking the boy from Rosie, the police gave Rosie another abandoned child to care for!

A sense of panic came over Rosie. She wasn't working and couldn't afford to care for two malnourished children. Her mind raced with possibilities, including abandoning the kids on the side of the road for someone else to look after.

In all this panic, Rosie was overcome with a sense of peaceful clarity. She knew she should and would take care of these children. From that moment on, Rosie's heart continued to endlessly expand.

"Some of us are here on earth to [help those who] need our guidance to face the challenges of life. Let your own light shine so [it] give[s] [light to others], too. [When you] liberate yourself from your own fear, [y]our presence automatically liberates others." - Rosie Mashale

Foundations across the world were contacted for support, and soon Rosie was able to buy the land next to her house. Children started flocking to "Mama Rosie" and Baphumelele, where there was healthcare, education, and housing facilities. Over 5,000 children have been helped by Rosie and her group of employees and volunteers.

Rosie quickly understood that you often can't wait for others to help in ways you yourself can help. She took matters into her own hands and dedicated her life to helping children have a fighting chance to reach their undeniable potential.

"In life, people tend to wait for good things to come to them. And by waiting, they miss out.

Usually, what you wish for doesn't fall in your lap; it falls somewhere nearby, and you have to recognize it, stand up, and put in the time and work it takes to get to it.

This isn't because the universe is cruel. It's because the universe is smart. It has its own cat-string theory and knows we don't appreciate things that fall into our laps."

Chapter 23

You Gotta Have Heart

The parents of newborn Austin Prario stood in shock as doctors told them their son's heart had leaks and one of its four chambers was inoperative. After three open-heart surgeries to correct his rare congenital heart condition, it was a miracle he was even alive. Austin's dad decided to run in the 1998 Boston Marathon to raise money for the children's hospital that was treating his son. His electric yellow shirt that read "you gotta have heart" was proudly displayed as he ran across the marathon's finish line that year.

Austin was repeatedly told by doctors that he was always going to be slower and weaker than his peers, and that competitive sports were out of the question for him. Austin took these remarks more as motivation than fact.

Austin's parents never pushed him, but they also never discouraged him. That's why he was allowed to run cross-country in the fourth grade, even when he came in dead last for every single race. That's also why they said he could play football and throw the javelin in high school. In high school, Austin started to discover that he could now not only keep up with kids his age, but he was also exceeding them in many sports. He even set his school's javelin record.

Austin's dad in the 1998 Boston Marathon

This motivation led Austin to want to see just how much he could really do, now that he knew how capable he was. So, Austin set out to complete the Boston Marathon, just like his dad had done when he was an infant. Austin's doctors said no, and that training with his heart condition would take at least two years, and even then, was likely not possible. So, Austin said "no" back. He started to quickly train so he could run in the Boston Marathon that year.

Austin's three open-heart surgeries and three working heart chambers didn't stop him from finishing the marathon that year. In fact, Austin finished in just over six hours. His race also helped him raise thousands of dollars for the same hospital he was treated at and that his dad had raised money for in 1998. Talk about coming full circle.

"It's cool to see this go full circle, from me carrying Austin across the finish line to this year," Austin's dad said. "It's neat to see someone turn a potential weakness into a strength to accomplish their goals."

The limitations we set ourselves define us unless we're constantly pushing away boundaries and self-made excuses.

"This is for all the people that said I could do it and for all the people that said I couldn't."- Austin Prario

A 20-year research study found that each happy friend who lives near you increases your chance of being happy by 25 percent.

A friend of your friend leads to a nearly 10 percent increase, and a friend of that friend has a 5.6 percent increased chance of happiness.

For comparison, having an extra $5,000 in income (in 1984 dollars) increased the probability of being happy by about 2%. Therefore, someone you don't know and have never met, the friend of a friend of a friend, can have a greater influence on your happiness than thousands of extra dollars.

Chapter 24

Veterans Who Surf

As he got off the plane, Andrew was overcome with a wave of emotion. Andrew Manzi had just finished his second deployment in Iraq with the United States Marine Corps. In battle, Andrew assumed he was never going to make it back home. Now back in Connecticut, he realized how much of the war he had brought back with him.

Andrew had suffered a brain injury and was struggling with post-traumatic stress disorder. He was merely managing to survive day by day. This changed the day he decided to poke around at a yard sale. An old surfboard caught his attention and he decided he was going to teach himself how to surf.

Surfing suddenly reminded Andrew of how it felt to be alive and liberated. This sense of freedom led Andrew to move to the sun-drenched beach and start teaching surfing lessons. Andrew felt empowered to try helping other veterans experience the healing powers of the open ocean. This is when he started the Warrior Surf Foundation.

The foundation offers free surfing lessons to veterans and their families. People struggling post-service have a unique opportunity to heal both mentally and physically. It gives the whole family a rare opportunity to bond and rebuild together. There are also therapy sessions on the beach with a licensed therapist.

"We all agreed that we need to really incorporate the whole family. So, if you want to come with your six kids, we can get them in the water. If you want to come out with your wife and surf, we have the babysitters so both of you can go in. I'm really a true believer on the whole community aspect of healing." – Andrew Manzi

Andrew found hope and peace out on the soothing ocean and has dedicated his life to bringing that peace to as many veterans as he can.

Professor Adam Grant defines 'givers' as people who contribute to others without expecting anything in return and preferring to give more than they get.

"In one study, pharmaceutical salespeople were assigned to a new product with no existing client base. Each quarter, even though the salespeople were paid commission, the givers pulled further ahead of the others. Moreover, giving was the only characteristic to predict performance: it didn't matter whether the salespeople were conscientious or carefree, extraverted or introverted, emotionally stable or anxious, and open-minded or traditional. The defining quality of a top pharmaceutical salesperson was being a giver. And powerless communication, marked by questions, is the defining quality of how givers sell."

Chapter 25

Fourteen Cows

The Maasai tribe of Kenya and Tanzania have a deeply preserved way of life and culture. The tribe is known for their semi-permanent homes made of sticks, mud, and compost, along with their sacred love of cattle. In fact, they even determine wealth and status by the number of children and cattle a person has.

The Maasai tribe are semi-nomadic, primarily located in Kenya and northern Tanzania

Kimeli Naiyomah grew up as a member of the Maasai tribe. He grew up without a father, his grandmother was murdered, and his mother was battling health ailments. Despite his hardships, Kimeli always dreamed of treating others, and decided he wanted to be a doctor.

The vision of becoming a doctor is a daunting battle for anyone, but especially for a Maasai. The tribe's traditions consisted of learning more practical skills such as cattle hurdling, cooking, and building homes. Kimeli didn't know anyone from his tribe who had gone to college, let alone medical school.

The Maasai tribe in Kenya

Realizing his dream of becoming a doctor required a structured high school education, Kimeli packed up a few belongings and went nine hours away to the closest school he could find. His fellow members of the Maasai tribe were so impressed by what he had accomplished that they helped gather $5,000 for him to go to medical school. Kimeli went on to the University of Oregon and then Stanford University Medical School.

On September 11th, 2001, Kimeli was in the heart of New York City when he witnessed the explosions. No part of his taxing upbringing had prepared him for that day. As a Maasai warrior, he was taught to never run away from tragedy, but to run toward it; but that day, there was nothing he could do to help so many people from losing their lives.

Eight months later, Kimeli made a trip back home to Kenya. The tragedy of 9/11 continued to cling to him. When he started sharing his story from that day, he realized that the tribe hadn't heard what had happened. Many of the Maasai tribe didn't have running water or electricity, let alone internet or telephones to learn about world events.

Despite their own lack of resources and wealth, the Maasai people wanted to help. The tribe decided to donate the possession they valued the most: their cattle. They put aside their own lack of resources to hold a ceremony in which they gifted 14 cows to the United States. The cattle were received by the deputy head of the United States Embassy in Kenya. Their selfless and tender gift stands as proof that you never have too little or an excuse not to help another.

"There is no nation so powerful it cannot be wounded, nor a people so small they cannot offer mighty comfort." – 14 Cows for America book

"For every $1 in extra charitable giving, income was $3.75 higher. Giving actually seemed to make people richer.

For example, imagine that you and I are both earning $60,000 a year. I give $1,600 to charity; you give $2,500 to charity. Although you gave away $900 more than I did, according to the evidence, you'll be on track to earn $3,375 more than I will in the coming year. Surprising as it seems, people who give more go on to earn more…

In a study…. people rated their happiness in the morning. Then, they received a windfall: an envelope with $20. They had to spend it by five P.M., and then they rated their happiness again…most people think they'd be happier spending the money on themselves, but the opposite is true. If you spend the money on yourself, your happiness doesn't change. But if you spend the money on others, you actually report becoming significantly happier."

Chapter 26

Peter Pan's Everlasting Gift

Since 1904, the magical story of Peter Pan has enchanted children and families worldwide. Peter Pan is the story of a young boy who stays young forever in the renowned Neverland. The story was created by James Matthew Barrie in London.

Barrie got the idea for the novel after being inspired by five brothers, known as the Davies brothers, playing in London's Kensington Gardens. Barrie's story of Peter Pan quickly captivated the hearts and minds of many, spreading to countless theater and cinema adaptions.

When the Davies brothers lost their parents, Barrie decided to finance their education, housing, and other costs, essentially becoming their guardian. Even after looking after these children, Barrie's generosity continued to flow.

Peter Pan was now a household name and generating a hefty amount of revenue. Barrie saw the future potential of what he had created and knew his story would last for generations to come. That is when Barrie decided to donate all his royalties to Great Ormond Street Children's Hospital in London.

Great Ormond Street Hospital in 1872 in London, England

Over 90 years later, money continues to flow into the children's hospital due to new Peter Pan movies and literary works. Barrie left not only the gift of a forever lively and youthful world, but the gift of forever helping sick children recover at Great Ormond Street Hospital.

"The moment you doubt whether you can fly, you cease forever to be able to do it." – Peter Pan by James Matthew Barrie

"We know from the now-iconic 1970s Good Samaritan study that the single greatest predictor of uncaring, unkind, and uncompassionate behavior, even among people who have devoted their lives to the welfare of others, is a perceived lack of time—a feeling of being rushed.

The sense of urgency seems to consume all of our other concerns—it is the razor's blade that severs our connection to anything outside ourselves, anything beyond the task at hand."

Chapter 27

Tangelo Park

The community of Tangelo Park in central Florida serves as a compelling example of the power of one individual. Tangelo Park has under 3,000 residents, and until 1993, was experiencing high crime with plummeting high school graduation rates. There was an influx of drugs, and no motivation for teenagers to apply to college or even finish high school. This impoverishment saw a whole new light with one individual's desire to give back to the town.

Harris Rosen was a self-made multi-millionaire who founded Rosen Hotels & Resorts in Orlando, Florida. When learning about Tangelo Park, Harris felt inspired to empower the youth and town. The Tangelo Park Program was created, and includes free preschool for all children, full Florida public college or trade school scholarships for every high school graduate, and a family resource center for parents.

"Epiphany might be too strong of a word...it was more of a voice. A feeling that 'now is the time.' You've achieved more success than you ever imagined. It's time now to recognize that you've been blessed...to be thankful and to share your good fortune with others." – Harris Rosen

The once dwindling town began to uplift itself. The high

school dropout rate fell from unacceptable levels to nearly 0%, and crime went down by over 80%. Not only were more students graduating, but they were working harder as well. Students' grades continually increased, and drug difficulties began to diminish in the neighborhood. It wasn't just the youth who were advancing, property values skyrocketed, and the neighborhood finally felt safe and warm to live in again.

When Harris first visited one of the community's elementary schools, he remembers asking the children how many of them wanted to go to college. Harris was heartbroken when only a couple of hands went up in response to his question. Now, Harris is heartened to say that when he visited these children after the Tangelo Park Program was implemented, every hand in the classroom shot up in excitement.

"I will be involved in the program until Tangelo Park is a gated community and the average home is selling for more than $1 million. Then I'm gone." – Harris Rosen

After decades and millions of dollars donated, Harris and the Tangelo Park Program continue to offer opportunities to hardworking individuals in the town. Harris also started an alternative spring break program where students from Cornell University volunteer to stay at one of Harris's hotels and mentor kids from the Tangelo Park Program's elementary school, middle school, and high school. The hope Harris has given has created a ripple effect of excitement in the community and given rise to so many young individuals being able to achieve their full potential.

In 2017, Harris initiated a second similar program in the urban downtown community of Parramore, Florida. Here, the community is significantly larger than Tangelo Park, and typically has more than 250 students in the Rosen Parramore preschool program. By setting this second example, Harris hopes other individuals who have the ability to do so will seriously consider creating similar programs in their own communities. Harris is absolutely convinced that by doing so, it will move us one step closer to his dream of changing America, one underserved community at a time.

The British Household Panel Survey revealed that an increase in the level of social involvement with friends and family is worth up to £85,000 a year in terms of life satisfaction.

To compare, it is worth more than getting married (£70,000 a year) and can compensate for half the loss in happiness from a separation (£170,000).

Chapter 28

Future Ties

After over 20 years as a Chicago police officer, Jennifer Maddox started feeling disheartened by the growing violence and gang activity in the city she so deeply loved. Jennifer recognized that a lot of the youth troubles stemmed from boredom and free time, not having role models, and a lack of proper education and motivational systems. On top of patrolling the streets, Jennifer knew she had the power to prevent some of these issues for children in Chicago from ever occurring.

Parkway Gardens Homes is famous for housing celebrities such as rapper Chief Keef and First Lady Michelle Obama. However, in recent years, the apartment complex had become even more well-known for its sky-rocketing crime rates. The housing is located on the border between multiple gang sites, making it a lethal and violent street.

In 2011, Jennifer convinced Parkway Gardens to open their basement for children to participate in activities and programs after school. She used her own money to fund a place where children and young adults could have a safe atmosphere to be tutored and acquire mentors. She called the idea Future Ties, in honor of encouraging at-risk kids to build their education and relationships to create a brighter future.

"Future Ties leads by example. Your voice matters and should be heard." – Jennifer Maddox

As Future Ties began to expand, Jennifer started to rely on parents and other role models in the community to help teach and advise the adolescents. As the number of people grew, so did the program's offerings. Future Ties now ran year-round, including during summer break. In addition to the traditional schooling and technology training, the program expanded to offer sports camps, trips to the beach, and talks on domestic violence and other challenges these children often face.

Many of these children grow up without a father, so there is immense power in being able to have a male mentor who is successful in their community. Jennifer is relentless in stopping these kids from believing they have no other option besides a life of crime and poverty. The members of Future Ties show up at student graduations, sports games, and any other activity the children are part of. They not only have access to more hobbies in their free time, but they also have a steady support system and positive influences to look up to.

"You can make more friends in two months by becoming interested in other people than you can in two years by trying to get other people interested in you."

Chapter 29

Friends, Not Customers

Two friends from Brisbane, Nicholas Marchesi and Lucas Patchett, believed every person had the right to dignity and basic hygiene. When the duo was 20 years old, they had the idea to build a free mobile laundry service for people experiencing homelessness.

They started going to laundry companies in the area to find one that would donate a washer and dryer. One of the local companies agreed, but told them there was no way they could get them working inside the van. After fitting the machines in their van, they quickly destroyed both the washer and dryer.

After extensive research, the pair quickly learned there was no other mobile laundry van that had ever been made. If they were going to make it work, they were going to have to figure this out on their own. They created new plans and asked the laundry company to donate another set of machines—these also broke. They made a third design and begged the company for one more donation of appliances, and thankfully, the third washing machine and dryer worked.

Orange Sky's laundry van

This win led to more wins. Nicholas and Lucas solved for getting power into their van, implementing a system for automatically applying laundry detergent, and handling the wastewater. The van began cruising around Brisbane and washing the clothes of people experiencing homelessness for free. The founders decided to call their non-profit Orange Sky, based on the song by Alexi Murdoch that sings of helping your sisters and brothers.

Orange Sky has since expanded to 31 locations across Australia, with more than 2,000 volunteers on board. Throughout this growth, Nicholas and Lucas continue to have one aspect of their business in common at all of their locations: conversation. The machines are all powered by technology and only take a few seconds to set up, which leaves a lot of idle time while the clothes are being washed. The time is used to have a conversation with people who are using the service. There is often music set up in the vans, and the Orange Sky volunteers take the time to sincerely get to know everyone. Orange Sky's business model doesn't acknowledge the people who use their service as "customers"; they are referred to as friends.

"At Orange Sky, we have a simple formula; we provide a platform for everyday Australians to connect through a regular and reliable service. The focus is on creating a safe, positive, and supportive environment for people who are too often ignored or who feel disconnected from the community.

One of the basic privileges a lot of us take for granted is having clean clothes to put on each day—it may seem small, but for a person doing it tough, having access to laundry and shower services can make a huge difference in their life.

Where we see our biggest impact is in the hours of conversation that take place between volunteers and friends while on shift. It is also about supporting discussions around everyone's role in helping people doing it tough through connection and genuine conversation." – Lucas Patchett

Two years after opening, Orange Sky expanded to open mobile showers as well. As the publicity and donations have grown, the company has expanded to New Zealand and hopes to eventually support people all over the world.

The vision of two 20-year-olds has amounted to more

than just helping the homeless feel clean, but helping them feel like they are part of their community once again.

"If I had my life to live over, I'd like to make more mistakes next time. I'd relax. I would limber up. I would be sillier than I have been this trip. I would take fewer things seriously. I would take more chances. I would climb more mountains and swim more rivers. I would eat more ice cream and less beans. I would perhaps have more actual trouble, but I'd have fewer imaginary ones.

You see, I'm one of those people who live sensibly and sanely hour after hour, day after day. Oh, I've had my moments, and if I had to do it over again, I'd have more of them. In fact, I'd try to have nothing else. Just moments, one after another, instead of living so many years ahead of each day.

I've been one of those persons who never goes anywhere without a thermometer, a hot water bottle, a raincoat, and a parachute. If I had to do it again, I would travel lighter than I have. If I had my life to live over, I would start barefoot earlier in the spring and stay that way later in the fall. I would go to more dances. I would ride more merry-go rounds; I would pick more daisies."

Chapter 30

Spider-Mable

There was finally a light at the end of the tunnel for six-year-old Mable who was ending her two-year battle with leukemia. During these two years, Mable had become captivated by Spider-Man. Spider-Man was brave and had radioactive blood, just like Mable after cancer treatments. Mable was granted any one wish from a children's charity that helps sick children. The decision was all too easy for Mable: she requested to be able to fight crime and be a superhero, just like Spider-Man.

One morning, Mable was abruptly woken up by her parents. Her parents informed her there was an urgent emergency and showed her a video. The video was of the police in Edmonton, Alberta, calling for Mable's help to solve a crime. The police announced that the Edmonton Oilers' star professional hockey player, Andrew Ference, was missing. Mable quickly threw on the Spider-Man costume her mom had made her and dashed out the door to save her beloved city of Edmonton.

A sparkling white limousine was waiting outside their house. The driver took Mable to her first stop, City Hall. Mable was greeted by Don Iveson, Edmonton's mayor. Don introduced Mable to Spider-Man, who was an actor all geared up in a Spider-Man costume. Spider-Man and

Don told Mable that the hockey player, Andrew, was kidnapped by a villain wearing a purple cape. The two of them implored Mable to help them save their beloved hockey star and town. A smile crept up on Mable's face as she nodded her head and eagerly accepted this task.

The next stop was Edmonton's large shopping mall. Here, Mable was greeted by police officers and hundreds of Edmonton locals who came to cheer Mable on her quest. Suddenly at the mall, the superheroes were alerted to a woman calling for Mable's help. The only catch was that the only way to reach the woman was by zipline! Mable fearlessly took a deep breath and swung across the room to save the woman. During this brave endeavor, there was a theme song made for Spider-Mable that played throughout the mall.

The town's media and other players of the Oilers hockey team now joined Mable to interview her. The superhero declared she wasn't scared to face the villain and was ready to save the hockey star. At this point, there were more celebrities and residents following and supporting Spider-Mable. There were even posts on social media from the 22nd Prime Minister of Canada, Stephen Harper, and Canada's current Prime Minister, Justin Trudeau, praising Spider-Mable. However, Mable's mission wasn't complete just yet.

After going through a ropes course, Mable finally found her last clue that led her to the town's zoo. Here, Spider-Mable spotted the villain and fired her web shooters at him. The villain fell to the ground, and the kidnapped hockey player was free! The town cheered and chanted thanks to Mable for saving the town.

The charity that granted Mable this day as part of her wish confessed that hers was the most elaborate wish they'd ever fulfilled. It took not only masses of planning, but for a whole town to come together and rally for Mable on her special day. All their efforts were worth it to make the six-year-old feel empowered and like the superhero she is.

"Only one trait consistently predicted presidential greatness after controlling for factors like years in office, wars, and scandals. It wasn't whether presidents were ambitious or forceful, friendly, or Machiavellian; it wasn't whether they were attractive, witty, poised, or polished.

What set great presidents apart was their intellectual curiosity and openness. They read widely and were as eager to learn about developments in biology, philosophy, architecture, and music as in domestic and foreign affairs… They saw many of their policies as experiments to run, not points to score."

Chapter 31

Don't Judge a Book by Its Cover

It's often easy to find only like-minded and similar individuals in our day-to-day routines. An event that started in Copenhagen in 2000 attempted to change this. The movement was called Human Library.

Human Library is a concept where people act as live books and tell their stories to others. People can volunteer to be storytellers, or books, and share their experiences with others in person. It's a way to break down barriers and step into someone else's shoes.

The live books come from varied walks of life. Examples include people who are soldiers, martial artists, or business owners along with those who are autistic or bipolar. Listeners, or readers, have the opportunity to feel what it's like to be someone so dissimilar than themselves. Readers are also encouraged to freely ask questions.

The first event was so impactful that the Human Library has quickly spread around the world. There have been more than 80 countries that have held a Human Library event. Thousands of people from each corner of the world have gained the opportunity to speak unreservedly with someone they might never have otherwise interacted with or understood.

"People are curious by nature, and through the conversations in the Human Library, I hope that readers become more open...and doesn't think in terms of 'us' and 'them' because I just want to be myself even though my story is different." – Human Library "book" volunteer

People can feel polarized and apart from others who live their lives differently. Hearing others' stories starts swapping prejudices with more empathy and tolerance for others. For all the dissimilarities between people, we always have more in common than everything keeping us apart.

"Think about the world. War, violence, natural disasters, man-made disasters, corruption. Things are bad, and it feels like they are getting worse, right? The rich are getting richer and the poor are getting poorer, and the number of poor just keeps increasing; and we will soon run out of resources unless we do something drastic. At least that's the picture that most...carry around in their heads. I call it the overdramatic worldview. It's stressful and misleading.

In fact, the vast majority of the world's population lives somewhere in the middle of the income scale. Perhaps they are not what we think of as middle class, but they are not living in extreme poverty. Their girls go to school, their children get vaccinated, they live in two-child families, and they want to go abroad on holiday, not as refugees. Step-by-step, year-by-year, the world is improving. Not on every single measure every single year, but as a rule. Though the world faces huge challenges, we have made tremendous progress. This is the fact-based worldview."

Chapter 32

Detroit Pioneer

The legacy of Mike Ilitch remains with the city of Detroit, Michigan. Little Caesars Pizza was founded by Mike, with headquarters that remain in Detroit. Mike went on to buy the Detroit Red Wings hockey team and the Detroit Tigers baseball team. Mike also started several non-profit foundations to help the residents of the city he so deeply treasured face problems such as hunger or veterans returning to civilization. Although Mike left behind this big legacy, one of his boldest acts of kindness was toward Rosa Parks, which remained a secret for years.

Rosa Parks was a pioneer of the Civil Rights Movement, known for refusing to give up her seat on a bus because of her skin color in 1955. Two years later, she moved to Detroit, where she resided for the remainder of her life. When Rosa was 81 years old, she was the victim of a robbery and assault in her home. A federal judge worked to find the exemplary activist a safer home in the city.

The fact that someone who helped change the landscape of racial tensions and inequality was living in dangerous conditions didn't sit well with Mike. As soon as he heard of what had happened to Rosa, he contacted the federal judge and pledged to pay for her rent. This wasn't a cry for publicity; in fact, the public didn't know of this act of generosity until almost ten years later.

Rosa's rent was paid for until the apartment complex granted her free rent during her last year. It's clear that Mike aided in transforming Detroit; yet, the most noble and genuine accomplishment remains his private efforts to support an American icon.

"The people who survive stress the best are the ones who actually increase their social investments in the middle of stress, which is the opposite of what most of us do.

Turns out that social connection is the greatest predictor of happiness we have when I run them in my studies. When we run social support metrics, they trump everything else we do, every time."

Chapter 33

Chocolate Bar

Dylan and Jonah met in preschool and have been best buds ever since. Since birth, Jonah has suffered from Glycogen Storage Disease Type 1B, a liver disorder that affects only one in a million people. Jonah was used to getting funny stares and glances when he had to regularly prick himself to check his blood sugar levels, but not from Dylan. Dylan loved Jonah and would try to make him laugh during all his medical checks.

When Dylan and Jonah were in first grade, Dylan started to learn more about Jonah. One day, while riding home in the car, Dylan's mom revealed how serious Jonah's condition was. She explained how Jonah couldn't have sleepovers because he had to have a cornstarch mixture every few hours, even at night, or he could go into seizures or worse. Hesitantly, she then told her son how there was also no cure, partly due to a lack of funding because of how rare and unheard of the disease was. Cutting his mom off, Dylan told her he was going to help.

The two boys loved pretending the word "chocolate bar" meant "awesome." For instance, they used to describe Disneyland or recess as being "chocolate bar." Now, with the hope of raising money to help his friend, Dylan decided he was going to write and sell a book. The title of the book? *Chocolate Bar*.

At six years old, Dylan wrote and published the children's book Chocolate Bar. The book described things he thought were awesome. Each penny of the proceeds was going to go to Glycogen Storage Disease Type 1B research.

> This book is dedicated to my friend Jonah. All money made will be donated to the Jonah pourhasarian FUND. Thank you for your GSD help.

Dylan's dedication from his Chocolate Bar book

The book was first sold at the boys' school. Dylan ran around the school and neighborhood, telling anyone who would listen about the book. On the first day, over $5,000 was raised for the cause. A bookstore then invited them to a book reading to tell their story and sign books. Swiftly following the reading, news outlets started getting ahold of the story, too.

In merely two years, the book was selling in 60 countries and thousands of copies had been sold. Dylan's love for his best friend had amounted to raising over one million dollars in this time. Jonah's doctor at the University of Connecticut's School of Medicine is one of the leading researchers working on a cure. Up until the 1970s, this disease was fatal. Now, the carrier virus that can deliver the missing gene in patients has been identified. A cure for Jonah and others is finally within reach. However, Dylan says he won't be done working until the day the cure is found, and he and his best friend can finally have their first big slumber party.

"When you have a bad day, a really bad day, try and treat the world better than it treated you."

Chapter 34

King Karma

Desperate times don't have to call for desperate measures. A Chinese student was visiting a friend in Boston when he stopped at a local tech store. When leaving the store, he suddenly realized he couldn't find his backpack. A sense of urgency and panic rushed over him as the backpack contained his passport, over $2,000 in cash, and almost $40,000 in traveler's cheques. He ran to the local police station to report the missing backpack, but was sure that he would never see his valued possessions again.

In the meantime, a homeless bystander was at the strip mall and found the student's missing backpack. Without a second thought, he immediately returned it to the police station without keeping a dime for himself. The police honored this selfless act by giving the finder a plaque, and several reporters wrote about the story. The man stated in interviews that no matter his circumstances, the thought of keeping the money would never have been an option for him.

Hundreds of miles away in Virginia, 27-year-old Ethan Whittington read about this story and decided a plaque wasn't enough for the man's altruism. Despite the fact he'd never met the man in the article or even been to Boston, Ethan approached friends and family to raise a few hundred dollars to help the generous man he had read about.

Word of Ethan's fundraiser started spreading all over the world. Donations from strangers reached over $160,000. A trust was created for the hero to ensure all the money went specifically toward his housing and other living expenses. Ethan even had the opportunity to fly out and meet the man he had been working so hard to support. Sometimes, helping strangers has good karma.

"He kept saying, 'Thank you.' You've got to continue to remind him that he is one who should be thanked, and he is the one who inspired people around the world because of his good deed." – Ethan Whittington

"A lot of you know the story of the two salesmen who went down to Africa in the 1900s. They were sent down to find if there was any opportunity for selling shoes, and they wrote telegrams back to Manchester.

And one of them wrote, 'Situation hopeless. Stop. They don't wear shoes.'

And the other one wrote, 'Glorious opportunity. They don't have any shoes yet.'"

Chapter 35

Rolling Books

In war-torn Afghanistan, most people don't have access to a quality education. One of the regions where education is especially lacking is Bamiyan, located in central Afghanistan. In 2012, the average estimated number of years of schooling for adults ages 25 to 59 in Bamiyan was 1.59 years for males and 0.27 years for females. Saber Hosseini, a schoolteacher in Bamiyan, has devoted his life to changing this statistic.

Saber recognized the importance of getting the population literate. This was often a daunting task due to limitations on funding for books and having educated teachers. Nonetheless, Saber gathered enough money to buy 200 books. Because of the harsh terrain and limited access to vehicles, Saber tirelessly rode to remote villages in Bamiyan on his bicycle, delivering the books to children. Saber rode for miles and miles through the blistering heat and snow to distribute as many books as he could.

The remote bicycle library became so popular that it quickly expanded all over the region. With the help of other volunteers, Saber acquired thousands of books. Saber and the volunteers rode all over Bamiyan, where children and adults could have access to stories and learn to read. The first permanent library even opened in the area.

In addition to delivering books and opening libraries, Saber also talks to all the children to whom he bikes. He teaches the children the vital importance of tolerance. His mission is for children to grow up not hating others just because they have different customs or beliefs. There is a feeling of pride and intelligence instilled in these children that Saber hopes will alter the direction of the country.

Besides the constant money constraint, there are other battles Saber faces. Saber and his wife have received multiple threats from extremist groups in the country. These groups only want people to read Islamic books with no interference from other ways of life. Despite these extreme dangers, Saber continues to fight for education and a better life for the children.

"My country has many problems. I have personally experienced those problems in my life. Poverty, displacement, [and] war are some of the problems that the people of Afghanistan have experienced. I have also suffered from some of these problems.

For example, when I was little, I had a brother named Server. He was younger than me. My father was a government employee. When the revolution took place there, everyone fled. We also escaped and went to a village around Bamiyan. It was winter there. The first days were very difficult for us. I was not familiar with the children of that village and I only played with my brother. He later caught a cold there. Every day, I waited for him to get well and play again. One afternoon, he got worse. In the middle of the night, he moaned a lot. I had just woken up when my mother cried and told my father that he was free. My mother and father cried softly. I found out that my brother died. I cried in bed, too. This great pain in my life was never forgotten.

I thought to myself many times, why do people suffer so much here? Why do he and the rest of the people just die from a cold? All this has a problem, and that is the lack of security. Security comes when people are educated. [This] motivated me to start my efforts to educate my community. In my opinion, the best thing for security and peace in Afghanistan is to educate the people, and that should start with children." – Saber Hosseini

"Work harder to appreciate your ordinary day."

Chapter 36

San Diego Highwayman

The year was 1964. Sixteen-year-old Thomas Weller was stuck in a blizzard while driving down the freeway past midnight. Suddenly, Thomas found he had no control over his car, which started veering off the road. The car slammed into a snowbank.

Covered with snow, Thomas and his vehicle were barely visible from the street. Before he had too much time to panic about if someone would ever find and help him, he heard a knock on his back windshield. A man helped pull Thomas out to safety. The only thing the stranger asked in return was for Thomas to pass on the favor. And so, he did.

Thomas soon converted his truck to resemble the Ghostbusters vehicle and started driving around the San Diego freeways, looking for people to help. Since Thomas worked as a mechanic and had training as an emergency medical technician, he was more than prepared to help stranded motorists.

When Thomas would find someone stranded on the expressway and no other help was coming, he would help the stranger repair their car and get to safety. His help included repairing vehicles, changing flat tires, providing gas, and offering rides.

Thomas and his "Ghostbusters" car

All of this help was done without asking for a single penny in return. With each motorist he encountered, Thomas would simply give them a business card that stated:

"Assisting you has been my pleasure. I ask for no payment other than for you to pass on the favor by helping someone in distress that you may encounter."

The pro bono roadside assistance carried on for over 50 years. Hundreds of panicked and helpless drivers have been relieved by Thomas. Thomas has driven thousands of miles and spent countless days in his white truck, trying to help strangers and get them to help others.

The San Diego Highwayman's efforts often came full circle. Thomas was once out patrolling the streets when he spotted a car stuck on the side of the road. When he pulled over, he noticed another Good Samaritan was already assisting with the accident. When Thomas asked the man why he had stopped to help, a soft smile came across his face. He told Thomas how a few months earlier his wife's car spun off the road and Thomas had been the one to help her. Obviously, his plea of asking others to pass on the favor had an impact.

"It is one of the most beautiful compensations of life that no man can sincerely try to help another without helping himself." - Thomas Weller's favorite quote by Ralph Waldo Emerson

"It was 1866, and the territory of Hawaii was 'fixing' its leprosy dilemma. Frightened of the disease, the authorities decided to exile lepers to the island of Molokai. There were sixteen...and they were strangers, not a family or a group of friends...

The ship returned two weeks later...and the crew was stunned by what they saw...The healthiest had not taken the food for themselves; they spent all their time caring for the weak...and every single one of the initial group was alive. The strong didn't do the 'rational' thing and choose selfish survival. They operated on instinct. Human nature. They made the seemingly irrational choice to care.

A 'just-so' story? Hardly...University of Pennsylvania professor Paul Robinson and Sarah Robinson explain that this response has been seen over and over in groups that find themselves in the most dire of situations, all around the world, all throughout history. Not always, but very often. Because 'irrational' cooperation is what led to our success as a species...If we didn't cooperate more often than not, if we didn't take the gamble and choose to help when it didn't make sense, quite simply: you would not be here reading this. The Molokai leper colony actually was an island. But what it proves is that you and I are not."

Chapter 37

"James Bond of Philanthropy"

Charles "Chuck" Feeney lived in a rented apartment with his wife. He was known for loving local burger joints, wearing a $15 knock-off watch, and flying coach with his reading materials stuffed in a small plastic bag.

On the outside, Chuck Feeney seemed like an ordinary man, which is why the fact that his net worth once exceeded 8 billion dollars comes as a surprise to many people.

Chuck grew up in New Jersey during the Great Depression. His parents were Irish American, blue-collar, hardworking role models. Working tirelessly as a young entrepreneur, Chuck co-founded Duty Free Shoppers Group in 1960. Duty Free Shoppers Group began to dominate airports, stores, and resorts around the globe, offering tax-free shopping for travelers.

Duty Free Shoppers Group blossomed into an empire. The business was employing thousands worldwide, and had expanded to offer a variety of diverse consumer products. On top of this, Chuck was also an astute investor. He was known for heavily investing in technology startups. The results of being a successful entrepreneur and investor led to Chuck's eventual billionaire status.

The billionaire believed he had more money than he or his family needed. Without announcing the news to the public, he quietly created the Atlantic Philanthropies. The Atlantic Philanthropies was a private foundation set up to help give Chuck's fortune away. Chuck lived by his mantra "giving while living" and believed there was no better time than now to begin contributing to others.

The philanthropy's reach extended far and wide. Donations were made to educational institutions, medical advancements, ecosystem research, and human rights support. His contributions extended to places like Vietnam, Australia, South Africa, and Ireland. Billions of dollars from Chuck's fortune have been given away through the Atlantic Philanthropies.

"Money has an attraction for some people, but you can't wear two pairs of shoes at one time." – Chuck Feeney

Not only did Chuck give away most of the money he had already made, but he also decided to part with his future income as well. Therefore, in 1984, Chuck decided he wanted to give away all his ownership of Duty Free Shoppers Group to the Atlantic Philanthropies. This was done so privately that at the time, his own business partners didn't even know that he had sold off his entire stake in the company.

Chuck was no longer a billionaire, or even close, after giving away over 99.9% of his money. He wanted his five children to learn the value of working diligently and earning their own wealth. Most importantly, he didn't believe he needed a fortune in order to live happily. It wasn't until years later that the world found out about

Chuck's generosity, which is why he has been coined the "James Bond of Philanthropy." This altruistic mindset has inspired many other wealthy individuals, including Bill Gates and Warren Buffett, who have credited Chuck as an inspiration for their various charities and foundations. However, none of Chuck's generosity was done for recognition, but because he had more of a desire to help others than to help only himself.

"All joy in this world comes from wanting others to be happy, and all suffering in this world comes from wanting only oneself to be happy."

Chapter 38

Music Mends Minds

Carol Rosenstein's Christmas in 2013 began at dawn with an emergency 9-1-1 call to report her husband had gone missing. Her husband, Irwin, had Parkinson's and dementia, and he had wandered out of the house. After a storm of police and helicopters, Irwin was found merely wandering the town for a hot cup of coffee.

Before Irwin's diagnosis, the couple was known by family and friends as the Jetsteins; relentless travelers, never staying still for too long. Irwin's deteriorating memory had put a taxing strain on them. Medicines weren't working, and some were causing more confusion and aggravation. There was a dreary feeling of isolation that the house was feeling for the first time.

Light was brought back into Carol and Irwin's lives when he visited the local university campus and started playing piano with students. The music empowered Irwin. He not only became more aware, but also more talkative and hopeful. There were still difficult days, but Carol finally felt like she had her partner back. She finally felt like she had her life back.

Neurologists explained to Carol that this sharp change in her husband's behavior was due to how music interacts with the brain. Music helps to ease symptoms of Parkinson's disease by sharpening movement coordination through vibroacoustics, or through the body hearing sound vibrations. Music also increases dopamine and lowers cortisol hormone levels, which results in strengthened happiness and lower stress and tension. The magnitude and power music had was a remarkable gift that Carol knew she had to share with others.

Carol and Irwin Rosenstein

Carol started the non-profit, Music Mends Minds, to help others with neurodegenerative illnesses. The organization creates choirs and bands around the country that help individuals socialize and hinder their progression of these diseases. Carol has since helped hundreds of people find the same relief and improvement that she and Irwin found through music.

"Music Mends Minds. It surely does. Twice a week, [my husband] and I take off in our yellow Mustang convertible to a lovely church in Brentwood. Perhaps we are feeling

sad, or tired or confused. But once we take our places and start to sing, surrounded by colleagues, friends, and new acquaintances, all uncertainties fly out the window. We laugh, we cry, we feel joyous. We are happy. We are alive. We are human. We are here. Yes, Music Mends Minds. But it also mends hearts and souls." – Paula, the loved one of a Music Mends Minds participant

"When we meet someone new, we quickly answer two questions: 'Can I trust this person?' and 'Can I respect this person?'

In our research, my colleagues and I have referred to these dimensions as warmth and competence respectively... But we don't value the two traits equally. First we judge warmth or trustworthiness, which we consider to be the more important of the two dimensions... Because from an evolutionary perspective, it is more crucial to our survival to know whether a person deserves our trust. We do value people who are capable...but we only notice that after we've judged their trustworthiness."

Chapter 39

Wales Fundraising

Biking to work one day in southeast Wales, Dan Black was struck by a car. He was rushed to the hospital, where he suffered a stroke that paralyzed his lower body and one of his arms.

Longing for the days he was able to walk, play guitar, and not have to be in a wheelchair, Dan started raising money for a stem cell treatment that could help with his condition. Through the help of his community and charity events, Dan was able to raise 22,000 pounds for the procedure.

One morning, Dan received an article from his mom that shifted his thinking. The article was about a six-year-old boy who lived close to Dan and was born with cerebral palsy, a neurological disorder that impairs muscle coordination and movement. The cerebral palsy had left the boy unable to walk, and his family was raising money for orthopedic surgery to help his condition. Dan immediately sympathized and donated 1,000 pounds of his own money to the boy's campaign.

Days went by, and Dan couldn't stop thinking about this boy and how he'd never been able to run and play or feel like he fit in. Dan decided to donate all his raised funds—amounting to 22,000 pounds—to help the six-year-old afford his operation. The two had never met, but Dan thought his treatment had a better chance of success and wanted to help improve a child's life.

After two operations and physical therapy, the child started learning to walk on his own. On sports day at his school, he was able to run across the field for the very first time all by himself. He finally started to feel like he belonged, all thanks to Dan's gesture of putting a stranger before himself.

"Success is getting what you want.
Happiness is wanting what you get."

Chapter 40

Human Race

Rob Gomez took one last morning stretch before slipping on his running shoes and heading out the door. It was the morning of the Beach to Beacon race that Rob had been eagerly anticipating.

Rob had made a name for himself in the running community for years. He had finished in the top 40 people for two Boston Marathons and had finished first in the Maine Marathon. The stakes were again high as Rob was now trying to place first in the Maine resident division of today's race.

The officials began the countdown...3...2...1...and Rob took off, flying past the starting line.

His heart was beating faster and faster, anticipation building as Rob turned the last corner of the race. Here, he saw his greatest competitor, and the defending Maine champion, hunched over. The other runner was suffering from a vile heat stroke. In a split-second decision, Rob grabbed the racer and placed his arm over his own shoulder for support. Propping his competitor up, Rob began to run again. As the race's end approached, Rob boosted the heat-stricken man across the finish line ahead of himself. Rob had just intentionally lost his divisional title and $1,000 prize.

Rob Gomez during the 2017 Beach to Beacon race

Reflecting on this self-sacrificing act, Rob notes he hadn't wanted to win that way, with another runner who was sick and in pain. Rob had watched the other man run incredibly fast in that race, and he felt that man deserved the recognition. To Rob, it was instinct when you see someone in need to help them first.

"I think I did what I did at the time because I knew I personally would feel better about myself if I didn't pass [him] while he was struggling to get to his feet so close to the finish. Being respectful and kind makes me feel good, and I suspect it makes others feel good, too.

I gave up some prize money and a first-place position in my division for my decision, but I knew that money and that first-place trophy couldn't replace the feeling I get by helping someone else and doing the right thing. No amount of money or accolades is worth doing the wrong thing—it will nag at you, haunt you, and make you feel uneasy about yourself. Doing the right thing is the better choice every time, and being kind and respectful is always the right thing to do."- Rob Gomez

"The perception of impact serves as a buffer against stress, enabling employees to avoid burnout and maintain their motivation and performance…

In one study, [researchers] found that high school teachers who perceived their jobs as stressful and demanding reported significantly greater burnout. But upon closer inspection, job stress was only linked to higher burnout for teachers who felt they didn't make a difference.

A sense of lasting impact protected against stress, preventing exhaustion."

Chapter 41

The Street School

Every stoplight in Karachi, Pakistan, is filled with the bustling of children trying to sell knickknacks or asking for money. Parents often can't afford to send their children to school, or prefer the children round up extra cash instead.

Twelve-year-old Shireen Zafar was used to the constant begging of children, which is why one young girl who didn't ask for money came as a shock to Shireen. The young girl nervously approached Shireen one afternoon on the street. All the girl softly asked was if Shireen could teach her.

"Once I was reading an article on the internet and read that there is an estimated 10 to 15 million kids who are not getting any education in Pakistan. So, I wanted to teach them so that there would be no unemployment for them in the future. And they would be able to live a quality life that we are living...I want to make everyone enjoy their lives like the way we are doing." – Hasan Zafar

Shireen and her fourteen-year-old brother, Hasan, decided they had the power to start teaching these children. They believed every child deserved a proper education, not just the wealthy. The two siblings found a flat plot of sand near their home and gathered some chairs and tables. Five days a week in the evenings, they taught the children in Karachi. Students first learned the local language, Urdu, along with basic math and writing. Over time, children also learned English, exercise courses, and more advanced subjects.

The Street School class in session

As the number of children began to grow, so did the obstacles. Many of the parents didn't want their children coming to school if it meant they were giving up time that could be spent on the streets gathering money. Also, many students didn't have any transportation to get to the Street School each day. Shireen and Hasan started by asking their parents and others who believed in their mission for donations. This money was used not only for classroom supplies, but also for transportation, food, and financial support. There was a van that would pick up and drop off the pupils. There was also small financial aid given to all children who attended to entice parents who wanted their children to be working instead. Moreover, children received books, writing supplies, and food.

The siblings saw how hungry hundreds of children in Karachi were to learn. The school got so big that the duo hired more teachers and opened another location in their city to accommodate the high demand. Parents who never received an education were also invited to attend the Street School with their kids. Students went from not knowing how to properly hold a pencil to being able to write insightful papers.

The Zafar siblings didn't see their young age as a hindrance in creating change. The Street School has given hundreds of people in Karachi an education, a right that everyone deserves.

"Just pay close attention to what excites you and what drains you.

Pay close attention to when you're being the real you and when you're trying to impress an invisible jury."

Chapter 42

Adopt a Student

Eighty-three-year-old Dora and twenty-six-year-old Maria are two of 650 pairs of roommates who have been matched up in Milan, Italy. Dora and Maria have dinner together every evening in their apartment while Dora tells Maria stories of her past and Maria makes Dora laugh with tales of her days at school.

The roommate-pairing started when Milan realized it had two problems. The first was their aging population, with many of the city's elders living alone. The second was expensive rent costs, with almost two-thirds of Milan's university students coming from outside the city. The MeglioMilano association decided the perfect solution was to pair these students with a senior who was living alone in a program called *Prendi in Casa uno Studente,* or "Adopt a Student."

Adopt a Student works by receiving applications from lonely seniors living alone in an apartment or house, along with applications from university students looking for accommodation in Milan. The students can live rent-free with these seniors, just paying fees to cover expenses. Seniors get help around the house and with costs while students get free accommodation close to their universities.

As Adopt a Student has expanded throughout the city, a gap has been bridged between the two generations. Youths have the opportunity to learn from a different generation while having a reliable and peaceful home. The roommates share book, movie, and wine recommendations and get to learn from someone so different from themselves.

Unlikely friendships are emerging all over Milan as Adopt a Student continues to grow.

References

Introduction
1. Jones, JoAnn C. Brockville Ontario.

Chapter 1
2. *Fight for the Forgotten*, www.fightfortheforgotten.org.
3. Wren, Justin. Instagram, 5 Apr. 2019.
4. Wren, Justin. "Fighting for Freedom." TED. TEDxWarwick. Apr. 2016.
5. "Best Things About Being Blind." Performance by Tommy Edison, The Tommy Edison Experience, 3 July 2012.

Chapter 2
6. "Be My Eyes - See the World Together." *Be My Eyes*, www.bemyeyes.com.
7. Jørgen Wiberg, Hans. "Skype Interview with Hans Jørgen Wiberg." 16 Aug. 2018.
8. Breznitz, Shlomo, and Collins Hemingway. *Maximum Brainpower: Challenging the Brain for Health and Wisdom*. Ballantine Books Trade Paperbacks, 2013.

Chapter 3
9. Omli, Jens. *Stone Kyambadde of the Wolves Soccer Club (Lost 2007 Interview)*. Performance by Stone Kymabadde, 27 Jan. 2014.
10. "The Power of Forgiveness." *Cornerstone Development Publications*, Dec. 2015.
11. Covey, Stephen. *The 7 Habits of Highly Effective People*. Free Press, 1989.
12. Kendall, R. (n.d.). *Stone Kyambadde*.
13. Dickens, Charles. *Doctor Marigold*. 1948.

Chapter 4
14. "Strangers Used Sign Language to Make His Day Easier, His Final Reaction Was Priceless." *Digital Synopsis*, Sept. 2015.

References | 165

15. "Hearing Hands - Touching Ad by Samsung." Digital Synopsis, Mar. 2015.
16. Tolle, Eckhart. *The Power of Now: A Guide to Spiritual Enlightenment*. 1997.

Chapter 5

17. Shriver, Maria. *The Heart of Nuba Official Trailer*. Performance by Tom Catena, The Heart of Nuba, Feb. 2018.
18. "A Conversation with Dr. Tom Catena." *Cmmb Volunteer Blog*, Cmmb, May 2017.
19. Catena, Tom, and Laura Manni. "Dr. Tom Catena is The Heart of Nuba." Cmmb, Apr. 2018.
20. *The Heart of Nuba*, www.theheartofnuba.com/.
21. Reeves, Eric, and Tom Catena. "An Interview with Dr. Tom Catena Concerning the Nuba Mountains, and a Humanitarian Update on the Region." *Sudan Research, Analysis, and Advocacy*, Mar. 2013.
22. Achor, Shawn, and Eric Barker. "Be More Successful: New Harvard Research Reveals A Fun Way To Do It." Barking Up The Wrong Tree, 28 Sept. 2014.

Chapter 6

23. "Telling Her Story: Khadijah Williams '13." *Harvard Alumni*, Dec. 2016.
24. Williams, Khadijah. *Essence 40th Anniversary Celebration Phenomenal Woman*, Essence, Aug. 2010, www.jeannineamber.com/uploads/cgblog/id22/homeless_to_harvard.pdf.
25. *Powers*. Lunarbaboon, 5 Mar. 2015, www.lunarbaboon.com.

Chapter 7

26. Gainer, Roland, and Avianne Tan. *Michigan Grandfather with Cancer Takes Up Uber Driving to Pay Off Home for Family*. ABC, Apr. 2015.
27. Covey, Stephen. *The 7 Habits of Highly Effective People*. Free Press, 1989.

Chapter 8
28. *Cambodian Children's Fund*, www.cambodianchildrensfund.org/.
29. Neeson, Scott. *Scott's Story*. Cambodian Children's Fund.
30. Grant, Adam. *Give and Take: A Revolutionary Approach to Success*. Viking, 2013.

Chapter 9
31. Wartman, Mason. 16 Feb. 2018.
32. Walmsley, Katie. *How to Make Money with $1 Slices*. CNN, Feb. 2015.
33. Grant, Adam. *Think Again: The Power of Knowing What You Don't Know*. Viking, 2021.

Chapter 10
34. Cox, Jessica. Possible Thinking, www.jessicacox.com/jessicas-history/.
35. Yadav, Neetu, and Jessica Cox. *World's First Armless Pilot Flying with Her Feet: Jessica Cox*. An Abled Life, 2020.
36. Grant, Adam. *Give and Take: A Revolutionary Approach to Success*. Viking, 2013.

Chapter 11
37. Andraka, Jack. "A Promising Test for Pancreatic Cancer…From a Teenager." TED. TED2013. Feb. 2013.
38. Andraka, Jack. "Jack Andraka: The Teen Inventor on a Mission to Fight Pancreatic Cancer." IPO Education Foundation, May 2016.
39. Andraka, Jack. "Interview with Jack Andraka." 19 Feb. 2018.
40. Gilbert, Daniel. *Stumbling on Happiness*. Knopf, 2006.

Chapter 12
41. "Wake Forest Coach Gives Player Kidney." *ESPN*, Feb. 2011.
42. Walter, Tom. "Interview with Tom Walter." 13 Aug. 2018.

Chapter 13

43. United States Holocaust Memorial Museum, Washington, DC. *Nicholas Winton And the Rescue of Children from Czechoslovakia, 1938–1939*. Holocaust Encyclopedia.
44. *Nicholas Winton*. Jewish Virtual Library.
45. *Nicholas Winton's Scrapbook Image*. Yad Vashem Archives.
46. Seligman, Martin E.P. *Learned Optimism: How to Change Your Mind and Your Life*. Knopf, 1991.

Chapter 14

47. *Sean Swarner - Inspirational Speaker, Author & Adventurer*. www.seanswarner.com/.
48. No Barriers Podcast, and Sean Swarner. "Episode 15." No Barriers, Mar. 2019.
49. Khadka, Navin Singh. "Mt Everest Grows by Nearly A Metre to New Height." *BBC News*, BBC, 8 Dec. 2020.
50. *The Summit Challenge*, www.thesummitchallenge.com.
51. Roser, Max, and Esteban Ortiz-Ospina. "Global Extreme Poverty." *Our World in Data*, 2013.
52. "World Poverty Clock." *World Data Lab*.

Chapter 15

53. *Zipline Drone Responds, Saves A 9-Day-Old Baby in Hours*. DroneDJ, Dec. 2019.
54. Bastone, Nick. *Meet the Two-Year-Old Silicon Valley Startup That Beat Amazon to Creating the World's Largest Fully Autonomous Drone Delivery System*. Business Insider, Dec. 2018.
55. Rinaudo, Keller. "How We're Using Drones to Deliver Blood and Save Lives." TED. TEDGlobal2017. Aug. 2017.
56. Rosling, Hans, et al. *Factfulness: Ten Reasons We're Wrong About the World--and Why Things Are Better Than You Think*. Flatiron Books, 2018.

Chapter 16

57. *History of Salk*. Salk.

58. *Jonas Salk*, M.D. Academy of Achievement.
59. Salk, Jonas. "Interview with Edwin Murrow." *See It Now*, CBS TV, Apr. 1955.
60. Twist, Lynne. *The Soul of Money: Transformation Your Relationship with Money and Life*. W. W. Norton & Company, 2003.

Chapter 17

61. Harrison, James. "Interview with James Harrison." 28 Oct. 2017.
62. Criss, Doug. "He Donated Blood Every Week For 60 Years and Saved the Lives Of 2.4 Million Babies." *CNN Heroes*, CNN, Dec. 2018.
63. *Importance of the Blood Supply*. American Red Cross.
64. Boyce, Christopher J., and Alex Wood. "Therapy 32 Times More Cost Effective at Increasing Happiness than Money." The University of Warwick and the University of Manchester, 20 Nov. 2009.

Chapter 18

65. Fleck, Fiona. *Dixon Chibanda: Grandmothers Help to Scale Up Mental Health Care*. World Health Organization, May 2018, www.who.int/bulletin/volumes/96/6/en/. Bull World Health Organ 2018;96:376–37
66. Chibanda, Dixon. "Why I Train Grandmothers to Treat Depression." TED. TEDWomen2017. Nov. 2017.
67. *Dixon Chibanda, The Friendship Bench*. Hearts on Fire.
68. *The Friendship Bench Zimbabwe*, www.friendshipbenchzimbabwe.org/.
69. Cousins, Sophie. *Mental Health Care for All: How Community-Led Innovations Are Taking Root*. The London School of Hygiene & Tropical Medicine, Oct. 2019.
70. Kühl, Eike. *Depression? Why Not Sit Down with A Grandmother?* Falling Walls.
71. Turner, Jean. *Friendship Bench Image Provided by Jean Turner, Friendship Bench Media, Communications & Design*. Accessed 9 Jan. 2021.

72. Global Coalition on Aging, and Transamerica Center for Retirement Studies. "Journey to Healthy Aging: Planning for Travel in Retirement." 2013.

Chapter 19

73. Braun, Bob. *Braun: Modest Doctor Makes Major Difference in Haiti*. NJ Advance Media, Mar. 2019.
74. *Megan Coffee*. The French-American Foundation.
75. *Who Is on the Board*. Ti Kay.
76. Covey, Stephen. "90/10 Principle."

Chapter 20

77. Cliatt-Wayman, Linda. "How to Fix A Broken School? Lead Fearlessly, Love Hard." TED. TEDWomen2015. May. 2015.
78. *Linda Cliatt-Wayman*, Principal Wayman, www.principalwayman.com/.
79. Waldinger, Robert. "What Makes a Good Life? Lessons from the Longest Study on Happiness." TED. TEDxBeaconStreet, Nov. 2015.

Chapter 21

80. *Fight like a Dog: The TEDx Talk of Rakesh Shukla*. Stronger with Rakesh Shukla, Apr. 2017.
81. Acuff, Jon. *Quitter: Closing the Gap Between Your Day Job & Your Dream Job*. Ramsey Press, 2011.

Chapter 22

82. Mashale, Rosie. "Interview with Rosie Mashale." 15 Mar. 2018.
83. Baphumelele, www.baphumelele.org.za/.
84. Habamenshi, Um'Khonde Patrick, and Llon Imanzi. *Rosie Mashale of South Africa - A Sentinel of Hope for A Community in Need*. The UMURAGE Foundation, Aug. 2018.
85. Strauss, Neil. *The Game: Penetrating the Secret Society of Pickup Artists*. 2005.

Chapter 23

86. Fox, Kit. *Three Open Heart Surgeries Later, Teen Is Running Boston*. Runner's World, Apr. 2017.
87. Prario, Austin. *Boston Marathon Image*. Accessed 19 Jan. 2021.
88. Fowler, James H, and Nicholas A Christakis. "Dynamic spread of happiness in a large social network: longitudinal analysis over 20 years in the Framingham Heart Study." *BMJ (Clinical research ed.)* vol. 337 a2338. 4 Dec. 2008, doi:10.1136/bmj.a2338

Chapter 24

89. Warrior Surf Foundation, www.warriorsurf.org/.
90. Dunn, Meghan. "Vets Use Unconventional Therapy to Treat PTSD." *CNN Heroes*, CNN, Dec. 2017.
91. Grant, Adam. *Give and Take: A Revolutionary Approach to Success*. Viking, 2013.

Chapter 25

92. Deedy, Carmen Agra, et al. *14 Cows for America*. 2009.
93. "Kenyan Masai Donate Cows to US." *BBC News World Edition*, BBC News, June 2002.
94. Lacey, Marc. *Where 9/11 News Is Late, but Aid Is Swift*. The New York Times, June 2002.
95. Fallacia83. *Maasai Map PNG*. Feb. 2008, www.upload.wikimedia.org/wikipedia/commons/6/6b/MAASAI_MAP.PNG.
96. *Photo of People, Dance, Africa, Tribe, Men, Tradition, Traditional, Masai, Checkered, Red Clothes*. www.pxhere.com/en/photo/604012?utm_content=shareClip&utm_medium=referral&utm_source=pxhere.
97. Grant, Adam. *Give and Take: A Revolutionary Approach to Success*. Viking, 2013.

Chapter 26

98. Barrie, James Matthew. *Peter Pan*. 1904.

99. *JM Barrie.* Great Ormond Street Hospital.
100. *About - J M Barrie.* www.jmbarrie.co.uk/about.
101. Wellcome Library, London. Wellcome Images images@wellcome.ac.uk https://wellcomeimages.org The Hospital for Sick Children, Great Ormond Street, London: the main facade. Wood engraving by W. E. Hodgkin after D. R. Warry, 1872. 1872 By: Daniel Robert Warryafter: W. E. Hodgkin and Edward Middleton BarryPublished: - Copyrighted work available under Creative Commons Attribution only license CC BY 4.0 https://creativecommons.org/licenses/by/4.0/
102. Popova, Maria. "The Power Paradox: The Surprising and Sobering Science of How We Gain and Lose Influence." The Marginalian, 28 Sept. 2016.
103. Darley, J. M., and Batson, C.D., "From Jerusalem to Jericho": A study of Situational and Dispositional Variables in Helping Behavior". JPSP, 1973, 27, 100-108

Chapter 27

104. *Harris Rosen.* Tangelo Park Program.
105. *Tangelo Park Program.* Rosen Gives Back.
106. "Big Enough." *Pegasus Magazine*, University of Central Florida.
107. Barker, Eric. "This Is What Your Relationships Are Worth in Dollars." Barking Up The Wrong Tree, 19 Jan. 2012.
108. Powdthavee, N. (2008). Putting a price tag on friends, relatives, and neighbours: Using surveys of life satisfaction to value social relationships. The Journal of Socio-Economics, 37(4), 1459–1480. https://doi.org/10.1016/j.socec.2007.04.004

Chapter 28

109. Maddox, Jennifer. "Interview with Jennifer Maddox." 16 Aug. 2018.
110. Future Ties, www.futureties.org/.
111. Carnegie, Dale. *How to Win Friends and Influence People*. 1936.

Chapter 29

112. Orange Sky Australia, www.orangesky.org.au/.
113. Fleming, Sean. *Meet the Mobile Charity That Gives the Homeless Free Showers and Washes Their Clothes*. World Economic Forum, Nov. 2018.
114. "Orange Sky Laundry Van Image." *World's First Free Mobile Laundry Service for The Homeless Seeks Volunteers*, Coast Community News, June 2018.
115. Stair, Nadine. "I'd Pick More Daises." *Reader's Digest*, Oct. 1953.

Chapter 30

116. SpiderMable-Film Inc.
117. Pruden, Jana G. *Spider-Mable Takes on Cancer and Crime in Edmonton*. Edmonton Journal, Sept. 2015.
118. Grant, Adam. *Think Again: The Power of Knowing What You Don't Know*. Viking, 2021.

Chapter 31

119. Helverskov, Kristine. "Interview with Kristine Helverskov." 29 May 2018.
120. Human Library, www.humanlibrary.org/.
121. Rosling, Hans, et al. *Factfulness: Ten Reasons We're Wrong About the World--and Why Things Are Better Than You Think*. Flatiron Books, 2018.

Chapter 32

122. Levenson, Eric. "Little Caesars Founder Quietly Paid Rosa Parks' Rent for Years." *CNN US*, CNN, Feb. 2017.
123. Larimer, Sarah. *Mike Ilitch Was Famous for His Fortune. But His Surprising Connection to Rosa Parks Reveals Something More*. The Washington Post, Feb. 2017.
124. Barker, Eric, and Shawn Achor. "Be More Successful: New Harvard Research Reveals A Fun Way to Do It." *Barking Up The Wrong Tree*.

References | 173

Chapter 33
125. Siegel, Dylan. "Dedication." *The Chocolate Bar Book*.
126. *Chocolate Bar Book*, www.chocolatebarbook.com/.
127. Lantz, Erika. "So Chocolate Bar." *Kind World Podcast*, WBUR, Apr. 2016.
128. Stump, Patrick.

Chapter 34
129. Annear, Steve. *Fundraiser Started for Homeless Man Who Turned In $40,000, Passport*. Boston Magazine, Sept. 2013.
130. *Homeless Man Who Turned in Cash Learns He's Been Crowd-Funded*. USA Today, Oct. 2013.
131. Zander, Benjamin. "The Transformative Power of Classical Music." TED. TED2008, Feb. 2008.

Chapter 35
132. Hosseini, Saber. "Interview with Saber Hosseini." 12 Jan. 2021.
133. *Books for Afghanistan*, www.booksforafghanistan.org/.
134. *Afghanistan: Socio-Demographic and Economic Survey*. Edited by Dulcie Liambach, The Central Statistics Organization of Afghanistan, 2014.
135. Ginsberg, Nina. *The Afghani Teacher Who Bicycles Books to Rural Villages*. Bicycles Create Change, July 2018.
136. Rubin, Gretchen.

Chapter 36
137. Little, Joe. "Hundreds Pull Over to Help San Diego Highwayman." *NBC San Diego*, NBC, Nov. 2020.
138. "San Diego Highway Man Retiring After 50 Years." *ABC News San Diego*, ABC, May 2019.
139. Douglass, Elizabeth. "A Good Samaritan Travels the Freeway." *Globe Newspaper Company*, Los Angeles Times, July 2008.
140. "You Make a Life by What You Give - San Diego Highwayman." Performance by Thomas Weller, WheelsNotHeels, July 2017, www.youtube.com/watch?v=sgNk1TGSZ6w.

141. Foster, Brent. *The San Diego Highwayman.* Dec. 2014.
142. Foster, Brent. *San Diego Highwayman Image.* LA Times, July 2008.
143. Emerson, Ralph Waldo.
144. Barker, Eric. *Plays Well With Others: The Surprising Science Behind Why Everything You Know About Relationships Is (Mostly) Wrong.* HarperOne, 2022.

Chapter 37

145. Miller, Judith, and Chuck Feeney. "New York Times Interview." *New York Times*, Jan. 1997.
146. Bertoni, Steven. *Exclusive: The Billionaire Who Wanted to Die Broke ... Is Now Officially Broke.* Forbes, Sept. 2020.
147. Bertoni, Steven. *Chuck Feeney: The Billionaire Who Is Trying to Go Broke.* GatesNotes, Sept. 2012.
148. *Wealthy Philanthropist Donates Billions to Charities.* The Borgen Project, Oct. 2020.
149. *He Gave Away $600 Million, And No One Knew.* The New York Times, Jan. 1997.
150. Shantideva.

Chapter 38

151. *Music Mends Minds*, www.musicmendsminds.org/.
152. Namer, Paula. *Music Mends Minds Testimonials.*
153. Klairmont, Laura. "'The 5th Dementia' Uses Music as Medicine." *CNN Heroes*, CNN, Mar. 2018.
154. *Carol and Irwin Rosenstein Image.* 8 Jan. 2021.
155. Cuddy, Amy. *Presence: Bringing Your Boldest Self to Your Biggest Challenges.* Little, Brown, 2015.

Chapter 39

156. Pride of Britain.
157. Thompson, Melissa. *Two Years After A Wheelchair-Bound Hero Sacrificed His Dream of Walking Again to Give Him A Chance This Brave Little Boy Has Ditched His Walking Frame.* Wales Online, Aug. 2015.
158. Carnegie, Dale.

References | 175

Chapter 40

159. Burns, Jay. *'Tremendous Teammate' Rob Gomez '05 Forgoes Race Victory to Help A Fallen Runner.* Bates, Aug. 2017.
160. Gomez, Rob. "Interview with Rob Gomez." Apr. 2018.
161. WE3Pix, Jan. 2021.
162. Grant, Adam. *Give and Take: A Revolutionary Approach to Success.* Viking, 2013.

Chapter 41

163. Ghafoor, Hammad. *Young Heroes: Meet the Teenagers Running Street Schools in Karachi.* Dunya News, Aug. 2017.
164. Yzola, Alana. *Teens Founded A Street School for Pakistan's Homeless Kids.* Insider Inc., Mar. 2016.
165. *Peace Fund Radio.* June 2016.
166. *The Street School Image.* The Street School by Hasan Shireen, Oct. 2018.
167. Sivers, Derek. *Anything You Want: 40 Lessons for a New Kind of Entrepreneur.* 2015.

Chapter 42

168. Charlton, Emma. *Students in Milan Are Moving in With the Elderly to Fight Loneliness and Save Money.* World Economic Forum, Nov. 2018.
169. Ghiglione, Giorgio. *Student Loans Company: Milan's Age-Defying Solution to High Rents.* The Guardian, Nov. 2018.
170. MeglioMilano.

Printed in Great Britain
by Amazon